Shining Star C

Anna Uhl Chamot

Pamela Hartmann

Jann Huizenga

Longman

longman.com

Shining Star

Pearson Education, 10 Bank Street, White Plains, NY 10606

Vice president, director of instructional design: Allen Ascher
Editorial director: Ed Lamprich
Acquisitions editor: Amanda Rappaport Dobbins
Project manager: Susan Saslow
Senior development editors: Lauren Weidenman, Bill Preston
Vice president, director of design and production: Rhea Banker
Executive managing editor: Linda Moser
Production manager: Ray Keating
Senior production editor: Sylvia Dare
Production editor: Patricia W. Nelson
Director of manufacturing: Patrice Fraccio
Senior manufacturing buyer: Edith Pullman
Photo research: Kirchoff/Wohlberg, Inc.
Design and production: Kirchoff/Wohlberg, Inc.
Cover design: Rhea Banker, Tara Mayer
Text font: 12.5/16 Minion
Acknowledgments: See page 286.
Illustration and photo credits: See page 287.

Library of Congress Cataloging-in-Publication Data
Chamot, Anna Uhl.
    Shining star / Anna Uhl Chamot, Pamela Hartmann, Jann Huizenga.
        p. cm.
    Includes index.
    Contents: A. Level 1. — B. Level 2. — C. Level 3.
    ISBN 0-13-093931-5 (pt. A) — ISBN 0-13-093933-1 (pt. B) — ISBN
0-13-093934-X (pt. C)
    1. English language—Textbooks for foreign speakers.   [1. English
language—Textbooks for foreign speakers. 2. Readers.]   I. Hartmann,
Pamela.   II Huizenga, Jann. III. Title.

PE1128.C48 2003
428.2'4—dc21

                                                    2002043460

ISBN: 0-13-093934-X

Printed in the United States of America
1 2 3 4 5 6 7 8 9 10–RRD–08 07 06 05 04 03

About the Authors

Anna Uhl Chamot is professor of secondary education and faculty adviser for ESL in George Washington University's Department of Teacher Preparation. She has been a researcher and teacher trainer in content-based second-language learning and language-learning strategies. She codesigned and has written extensively about the

Cognitive Academic Language Learning Approach (CALLA) and spent seven years implementing the CALLA model in the Arlington Public Schools in Virginia.

Pamela Hartmann is a teacher and writer in the field of Teaching English to Speakers of Other Languages (TESOL). She has taught ESL and EFL in California and overseas since 1973. In addition, she has authored several books in the fields of TESOL and cross-cultural communication.

Jann Huizenga is an educator and consultant in the field of TESOL, with a special interest in teaching reading. She has worked as a teacher trainer at Hunter College in New York City, at the University of New Mexico at Los Alamos, and overseas. She has written numerous books for ESL students.

Consultants and Reviewers

Jennifer Alexander
Houston ISD
Houston, Texas

Heidi Ballard
University of California at Berkeley
Henry M. Gunn High School
Palo Alto, California

Susan Benz
Balboa High School
San Francisco, California

Lynore M. Carnuccio
esl, etc Educational Consultants
Yukon, Oklahoma

Wes Clarkson
El Paso ISD
El Paso, Texas

Lynn Clausen
Pajaro Valley USD
Watsonville, California

Brigitte Deyle
Northside ISD
San Antonio, Texas

Janet L. Downey
Riverside Unified School District
Riverside, California

Elvira Estrada
Socorro ISD
El Paso County, Texas

Virginia L. Flanagin
University of California at Berkeley
Berkeley, California

Leanna Harrison
Stinson Middle School
San Antonio, Texas

Gloria Henllan-Jones
Amundsen High School
Chicago, Illinois

Ann Hilborn
Educational Consultant
Houston, Texas

Terry Hirsch
Waukegan High School
Waukegan, Illinois

Kevin Kubota
Freeman High School
Richmond, Virginia

Betsy Lewis-Moreno
Thomas Edison High School
San Antonio, Texas

Caroline LoBuglio
Lower East Side Preparatory High
School
New York, New York

Jean McConochie
Pace University
New York, New York

James McGuinness
National Faculty – Lesley University
Yarmouthport, Massachusetts

Kaye Wiley Maggart
New Haven Public Schools
New Haven, Connecticut

Maria Malagon
Montgomery County Public Schools
Rockville, Maryland

Elva Ramirez Mellor
Chula Vista Elementary School
District
Chula Vista, California

Wendy Meyers
Casey Middle School
Boulder, Colorado

Linda Nelson
Century High School
Santa Ana, California

Jessica O'Donovan
Bilingual/ESL Technical Assistance
Center (BETAC)
Elmsford, New York

Patrizia Panella
Isaac E. Young Middle School
New Rochelle, New York

Kathy Privrat
Lower East Side Preparatory
High School
New York, New York

Jan Reed
Garden Grove USD
Garden Grove, California

Leslie S. Remington
Hermitage High School
Richmond, Virginia

Linda Riehl
Grady Middle School
Houston, Texas

Michael Ringler
Hialeah-Miami Lakes Senior
High School
Hialeah, Florida

Alma Rodriguez
Bowie High School
El Paso, Texas

Marjorie Bandler Rosenberg
Malrose Associates
Annandale, Virginia

Sandra Salas
Rayburn Middle School
San Antonio, Texas

Carrie Schreiber
International Newcomer
Academy
Fort Worth, Texas

Angela Seale
Independent Consultant
Houston, Texas

Penny Shanihan
Pearland High School
Houston, Texas

Katherine Silva
Holmes High School
San Antonio, Texas

Kathleen Anderson Steeves
The George Washington
University
Washington, D.C.

Trudy Todd
Fairfax Public Schools,
Emeritus
Fairfax County, Virginia

Sylvia Velasquez
Braddock Senior High School
Miami, Florida

Sharon Weiss
Educational Consultant
Glenview, Illinois

Ruth White
Washington High School
Cedar Rapids, Iowa

To the Student

Welcome to Shining Star

This program will help you develop the English skills you need for different school subjects. Each unit has selections about a variety of topics, including science, social studies, and math. There are also literary selections. These selections will help you understand the vocabulary and organization of different types of texts such as stories, poems, and nonfiction articles. They will give you the tools you need to approach the content of the different subjects you take in school.

Before starting to read a selection, you will do activities that help you relate your background knowledge to the new information in the text. You will also study some of the new words in the text to give you a head start as you begin to read. Finally, you will learn a reading strategy that will help you read with greater understanding.

While you read, ask yourself, "Am I understanding this? Does it make sense to me?" Remember to use the reading strategy! Your teacher may also play a recording of the selection so that you can listen to it as you read.

After you read, you will check your understanding of the text. Then you will work on activities to help improve your English skills in grammar, phonics, and spelling.

To extend your ability in English, you will participate in several types of activities related to the selections in each unit. Some of these activities involve listening and speaking, while in others you will produce different kinds of writing. Each unit also has a number of projects in which you can practice your artistic, musical, dramatic, scientific, mathematical, language, social, and thinking talents. You'll also see some suggestions for further reading related to the theme of the unit.

We hope that you enjoy *Shining Star* as much as we enjoyed writing it for you!

Anna Uhl Chamot
Pamela Hartmann
Jann Huizenga

Contents

PART 2

PUT IT ALL TOGETHER

UNIT 2

The Human Spirit

PART 2

PUT IT ALL TOGETHER

PART 2

PUT IT ALL TOGETHER

UNIT 4

Risks and Challenges

PART 1

PART 2

PUT IT ALL TOGETHER

UNIT 5

Reach for the Stars

PART 2

PUT IT ALL TOGETHER

UNIT 6

Shifting Perspectives

PART 2

PUT IT ALL TOGETHER

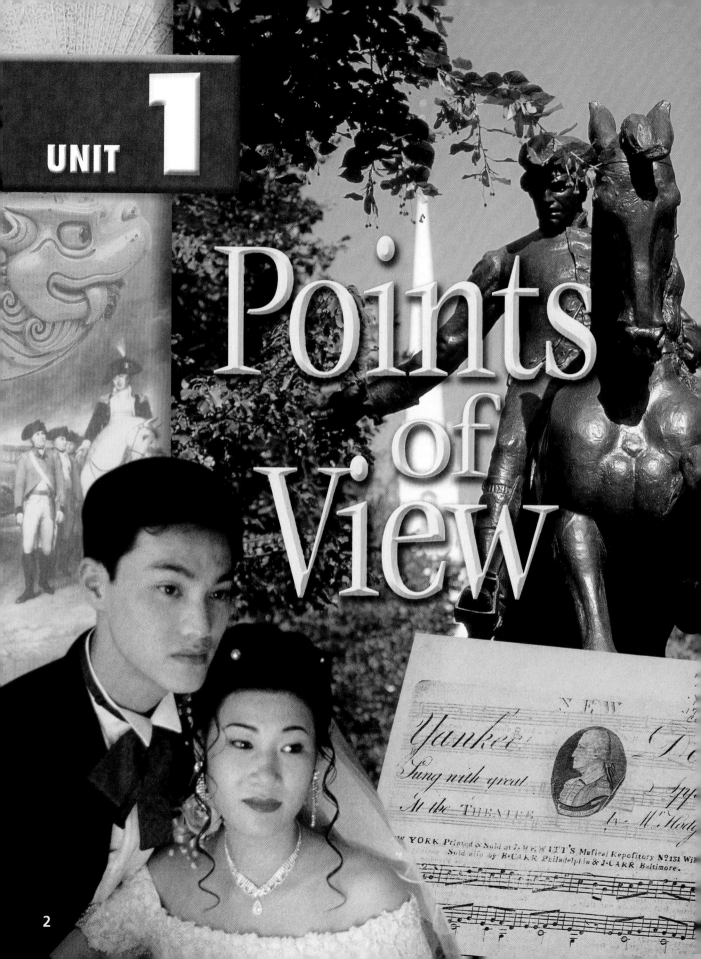

Points of View

PART 1

- "Moving Toward Independence: The Boston Tea Party"
- "Yankee Doodle"
- "The World Turned Upside Down"

PART 2

- From *Daughter of China*, Meihong Xu and Larry Engelmann
- "Understanding Cultural Differences," Sandy Cameron

Your "point of view" is how you understand, or "see," a situation. People have different points of view for many reasons. These reasons include differences in culture, family background, circumstances, and personality. When groups or people want to get along, it is important for them to try to understand each other's point of view.

In Part 1, you will learn how the different points of view of the American colonists and the British led to conflict, and eventually to the American Revolution. Then you will listen to two songs from that period, which show opposing British and American points of view of the same situation.

In Part 2, you will read about different points of view based on culture and language, family background, and personality. First, you will read a story in which people's points of view are influenced by their language and culture. Then you will read an article about understanding and respecting people's cultural differences.

Prepare to Read

BACKGROUND

"The Boston Tea Party" is a social studies article. It gives the background of an important event in early U.S. history.

Make connections During the 1600s and 1700s, Great Britain created colonies in North America. The British government forced the colonists to pay taxes. The colonists did not think this was fair. They did not have representatives in the British government. They had no control over how their tax money was used.

The colonists' anger led to the "Boston Tea Party." The Boston Tea Party was an important event in the conflict between the colonists and the British—a conflict that led to the American Revolution.

1. What are taxes? Think of some things that you buy. Do you pay taxes on these things?
2. How did the colonists feel about paying taxes?
3. What did the colonists' anger lead to?

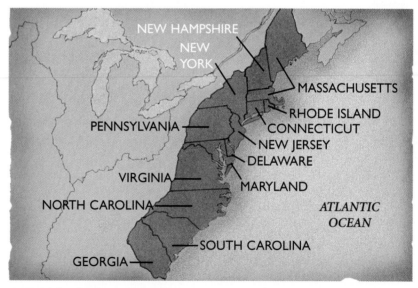

▲ British colonies in America

boycott
cargo
disguised
financial
independence
traitor
uproar

VOCABULARY

Read these sentences. Use the context to figure out the meaning of the **red** words. Use a dictionary to check your answers. Write each word and its meaning in your notebook.

1. The colonists refused to buy tea. The British were unable to sell any tea because of the colonists' **boycott**.
2. The colonists tried to prevent the ship from unloading its **cargo** of tea.
3. The men were **disguised** so that no one would know who they were.
4. The East India Company had **financial** problems and could not pay its workers.
5. The colonists didn't want the British to govern them. They wanted **independence**.
6. A colonist who supported the British was considered a **traitor** by the other colonists.
7. The colonists were very angry about the tax, and there was a huge **uproar**.

READING STRATEGY

Previewing

Previewing a text helps you understand it better. It also helps you establish your purpose for reading the text.

- To preview, read the title and look at the maps and illustrations. Then read the headings and the first and last paragraphs of each section. Sometimes it is helpful to read the first line of all of the paragraphs in the text.

- As you preview, ask yourself these questions: What will I read about? What do I already know about the topic? What questions might be answered in the text?

- Keep in mind your reasons for reading the text.

Moving Toward Independence:
The Boston Tea Party

The Colonists and Tea

In the 1770s, in the American colonies, people loved tea. Many colonists brewed tea twice a day. One British visitor said that people "would rather go without their dinners than without a cup of tea."

Colonists busy in their new settlement ▼

Uproar over Tea

The British East India Company supplied the colonies with tea. The company bought tea in southern Asia and sold it to tea **merchants**. The merchants then sold the tea to the colonists. They sold the tea at a higher price than they paid for it. The higher price included a tax that the British put on the tea.

One reason Britain taxed tea was to show the colonies that they were still a part of the British Empire. The tea tax was a small one, but the colonists **resented** it. They did not have a say in the British government. Why should they give the British government their money? They refused to buy the tea from the merchants. This caused serious financial trouble for the British East India Company. More than 15 million pounds of its tea sat unsold in British **warehouses** because the colonists refused to buy it.

merchants, people who buy and sell goods
resented, felt angry because something was not fair
warehouses, large buildings where things are stored

Tea arrived in America on merchant ships owned by the British East India Company. ▶

BEFORE YOU GO ON . . .

1 Where did the British East India Company buy tea?

2 Why did the colonists refuse to buy tea?

HOW ABOUT YOU?

- Do you think refusing to buy tea was a good way for the colonists to protest? What other ways could they have protested?

The Tea Act of 1773

The **British Parliament** tried to help the East India Company by passing the Tea Act of 1773. This act let the company sell tea directly to colonists. Although the colonists would still have to pay the tea tax, the tea itself would cost less than ever before.

To the surprise of Parliament, the colonists protested the Tea Act. Tea merchants were angry, too, because they had lost their **income** from the tea **trade**. If Parliament harmed tea merchants, they warned, it might also turn against other businesses.

Even tea drinkers, who would have benefited from the Tea Act, were against it. Colonists believed that it was a British **trick** to make them accept Parliament's right to tax the colonies.

▲ King George III and members of the British Parliament passed laws that affected the colonists.

British Parliament, the part of the British government that makes laws
income, money people earn
trade, activity of buying and selling goods
trick, clever act; deception

A Boycott

The colonists responded to the new tax with a boycott: The colonists stopped buying tea. One colonial newspaper warned:

> **Do not suffer yourself to sip the accursed, dutied STUFF.** For if you do, the devil will immediately enter into you, and you will instantly become a traitor to your country.

Patriotic groups led the boycott. They served coffee, or they made "liberty tea" from raspberry leaves. At some ports, they stopped the British East India Company from unloading cargoes of tea.

▲ After raspberry leaves were dried, they could be used to make tea.

Do not suffer yourself to sip the accursed, dutied stuff. Don't drink the bad, taxed tea.

patriotic groups, groups of people who were loyal to the colonists' side of the conflict

Cargo is unloaded from a ship. ▶

BEFORE YOU GO ON . . .

1 Why did the Tea Act make tea merchants angry? Why did it make the colonists angry?

2 How did the colonists respond to the Tea Act?

HOW ABOUT YOU?

● Have you ever had to give up something you liked for an important reason? Explain.

The "Boston Tea Party"

In late November 1773, three ships **loaded with** tea reached Boston Harbor. Sam Adams was a patriot who lived in Boston. Adams and a patriotic group called the Sons of Liberty wanted the ships to leave the harbor with the tea. The governor of Massachusetts, Thomas Hutchinson, **insisted** that the ships stay where they were.

On the night of December 16, the Sons of Liberty met in the Old South Meetinghouse. They sent a message to the governor demanding that the ships leave the harbor. When the governor **rejected** the demand, Adams stood up and declared, "This meeting can do nothing further to save the country."

Adams's words seemed to be a **signal**. A group of men disguised as Mohawk Indians burst into the meetinghouse. From the gallery above, voices cried, "Boston Harbor a teapot tonight! The Mohawks are here!"

▲ The Boston Tea Party

The disguised colonists left the meetinghouse and headed for the harbor. Others joined them on the way.

Under a nearly full moon, the men boarded the ships, split open the tea chests, and threw the tea into the harbor. By 10:00 P.M., the Boston Tea Party, as it was later called, was over.

---

loaded with, full of
insisted, said something that must happen or be done
rejected, said no to
signal, sound, action, or movement that tells you to do something

▲ John Adams

The Tea Protest Continues

John Adams was a colonial lawyer and patriot who would later become the nation's second president. He was also the cousin of Sam Adams. One night in July 1774, he stopped at an inn on his way home. He had ridden more than 30 miles and was covered with dust from the road. He was tired and very thirsty.

Adams asked the innkeeper for a cup of tea. The innkeeper refused to serve Adams any tea. She informed him that the inn did not serve tea. He would have to drink coffee instead.

Later, Adams **praised** the innkeeper for refusing to serve tea. In a letter to his wife, Abigail, he wrote that all colonists should stop drinking tea. He himself decided to drink no more tea.

BEFORE YOU GO ON . . .

1 How did the Boston Tea Party begin?

2 What did the disguised colonists do to the cargoes of tea?

HOW ABOUT YOU?

● Do you think the colonists were right to throw the tea into the harbor? Why or why not?

---

praised, said good things about

Review and Practice

Reread the text on the Boston Tea Party. Then copy the chart into your notebook and complete it.

Who	What They Did
Colonists	*responded to the Tea Act with a boycott*
Tea merchants	
British Parliament	
John Adams	
Sons of Liberty	

Work with a partner. Using your charts, tell about what the people or groups did.

◀ The Boston Tea Party Museum in Boston Harbor features a reproduction of a ship from the Boston Tea Party.

EXTENSION

Before the boycott, how did the tea get to the colonists? Copy the flowchart into your notebook. Complete it with words and phrases from the box. Then compare your flowchart with a partner's.

Merchants	**British East India Company** ~~colonists~~
British warehouses	~~South Asian tea growers~~

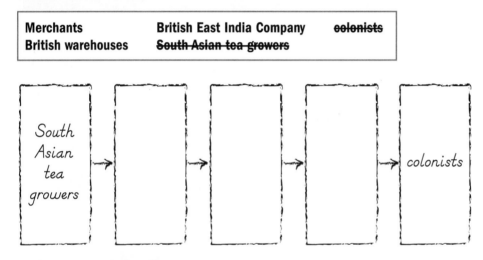

DISCUSSION

Discuss in pairs or small groups.

1. Why did the colonists feel that the tea tax was not fair?
2. Why did the Tea Act make the colonists angry even though it made tea cheaper to buy?
3. Imagine that you lived in Boston in the 1770s. Would you participate in the tea boycott? Why or why not?
4. Think about how you previewed the text. What did you do to preview? Which of your predictions about what you would read were correct?

Songs

The American Revolution inspired many works of art, literature, and music. The songs "Yankee Doodle" and "The World Turned Upside Down" show the different points of view of the colonists and the British. The timeline on page 15 will give you a brief account of the important events of the American Revolution.

Yankee Doodle

Father and I went down to camp,
Along with Captain Gooding,
And there we saw the men and boys
As thick as **hasty pudding**.

Chorus:
Yankee Doodle keep it up,
Yankee Doodle Dandy,
Mind the music and the step,
And with the girls be handy.

There was **Captain** Washington
Upon a slapping stallion,
Giving orders to his men,
I guess there was a million.

Repeat chorus.

---

hasty pudding, thick, sweet, creamy food
    popular during colonial times
Yankee Doodle, originally used by the
    British to mean "American fool," but
    adopted by the Americans as a way to
    refer to themselves
mind, pay attention to
Captain, military title meaning "chief"

▲ *Surrender of Lord Cornwallis* by
John Trumbull, showing the 1781
surrender of British troops led by
Cornwallis to an American army in
Yorktown, Virginia

Important Events of the American Revolution

Study the timeline.

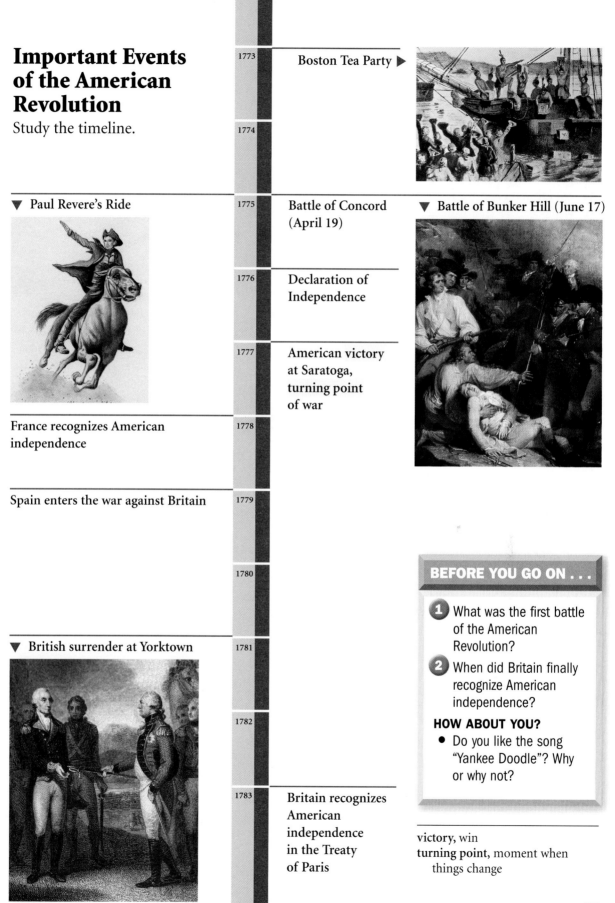

1773	**Boston Tea Party** ▶	
1774		
1775	**Battle of Concord (April 19)**	▼ Battle of Bunker Hill (June 17)
1776	**Declaration of Independence**	
1777	**American victory at Saratoga, turning point of war**	
1778	France recognizes American independence	
1779	Spain enters the war against Britain	
1780		
1781	▼ British surrender at Yorktown	
1782		
1783	**Britain recognizes American independence in the Treaty of Paris**	

▼ Paul Revere's Ride

BEFORE YOU GO ON . . .

1 What was the first battle of the American Revolution?

2 When did Britain finally recognize American independence?

HOW ABOUT YOU?

• Do you like the song "Yankee Doodle"? Why or why not?

---

victory, win
turning point, moment when things change

15

The World Turned Upside Down

If **buttercups** buzz'd after the **bee**,
If boats were on land, churches on sea,
If ponies rode men,
And if grass ate the cows,
And cats should be chased
Into holes by the mouse,
If the mamas sold their babies
To the **gypsies** for **half a crown**,
If summer were spring,
And the other way 'round,
Then all the world would be upside down.

---

buttercups, small plants with bright yellow flowers
    shaped like cups
bee, black and yellow insect that makes honey, using
    pollen from flowers such as buttercups
gypsies, group of people usually living nomadic life
half a crown, British coin (no longer in use)

About the Songs

No one knows who wrote "Yankee Doodle." One story tells that a British officer wrote it to make fun of the colonial soldiers. The colonial soldiers liked the song and adopted it as their own.

The composer of "The World Turned Upside Down," which was written in 1643, is also unknown. The British may have played it at Yorktown. From their point of view, the victory of the untrained group of colonists seemed crazy—as though the world was turned upside down.

BEFORE YOU GO ON . . .

1. What are two things the song says to illustrate the idea of "the world turned upside down"?
2. How do the words of this song express the British soldiers' point of view?

HOW ABOUT YOU?

- Do the words of the song seem playful or serious to you? Explain.

Link the Readings

REFLECTION

Read the texts of the songs again. Think about the Boston Tea Party text. Then copy the chart into your notebook and complete it.

Title of Selection	Genre	Fiction or Nonfiction	Purpose of Selection	Viewpoint
"Moving Toward Independence: The Boston Tea Party"				
"Yankee Doodle"	song		to entertain	
"The World Turned Upside Down"				British

DISCUSSION

Discuss in pairs or small groups.

1. Listen to the songs again. How are the songs similar? How are they different?
2. Do you know about another similar conflict in history? What happened? How were the events similar to the ones leading to the Boston Tea Party?

American soldier ▶

17

Connect to Writing

GRAMMAR

Using the Simple Past

We use the **simple past** to talk about an action that happened in the past and is completed.

> The colonists **brewed** tea twice a day.
> In the colonies, people **loved** tea.
> The tea merchants **lost** income.

For most regular verbs, add **-ed** to the base form to form the simple past.

> brew + -ed   **brewed**
> resent + -ed **resented**

For regular verbs that end with e, add **-d** to form the simple past.

> love + -d   **loved**
> refuse + -d   **refused**

Irregular verbs have special past forms. Review these irregular verbs and their past forms.

go	**went**	have	**had**
eat	**ate**	lose	**lost**
sell	**sold**	run	**ran**
pay	**paid**	fly	**flew**
sit	**sat**	win	**won**

For negative simple past sentences, use *did not* (*didn't*) + verb.

> Tea merchants **did not want** to lose their income.
> The colonists **did not accept** the Tea Act.
> The innkeeper **didn't serve** tea to John Adams.

Practice

Choose eight verbs from the charts. Write sentences in the simple past using the verbs. Then compare your sentences with a partner's.

SKILLS FOR WRITING

Using Sequence Words in Narrative Text

A **narrative text** tells a story. Most narratives focus on past events. The text usually tells about the events in chronological order. Writers often use **sequence words** to make the order of events clear.

Here are some sequence words that you can use to make the order of events clear.

yesterday	last week	first
second	third	at that point
soon	next	after that
then	finally	

Read this narrative text. Ask and answer the questions with a partner.

Jeremy Ng

The colonists were upset about the tax that the British put on tea. (First) they started a tea boycott. The boycott made it hard for the British to make money on tea. (Then,) when some British ships filled with tea came into the harbor, the colonists demanded that they leave. The British governor refused. (Finally,) the colonists boarded the ships and threw the tea into the harbor, ruining it. This was the "Boston Tea Party."

sequence words

1. What sequence words are there in the narrative?
2. Find the simple past verbs. Are they regular or irregular?
3. In your own words, retell the story. Use sequence words.

WRITING ASSIGNMENT

Narrative Paragraphs

You will write one or two narrative paragraphs about a historical event of your choice.

1. **Read** Reread the section "The Tea Protest Continues" on page 11 and the model narrative on page 19 for examples of narrative paragraphs.

Writing Strategy: Sequence-of-Events Chart

Before you begin to write, you can use a chart to help you organize your thoughts. Here is a chart the writer of the paragraph on page 19 used to help him select sequence words.

Possible Sequence Words	Event
first	The colonists started a tea boycott.
next, then, after that	They demanded that British ships leave Boston Harbor.
finally	They boarded the ships and threw the tea into the harbor.

---

2. **Make a chart** Make a chart in your notebook. Write each event in the right column. In the left column, write one or two sequence words that you can use to introduce the event.

3. **Write** Use your chart to help you write one or two narrative paragraphs.

EDITING CHECKLIST

Did you . . .

► check to see that your narrative has a beginning, a middle, and an end?

► check to make sure the events are in the correct order?

► use sequence words to show the order of events clearly?

► form and use simple past verbs correctly?

Check Your Knowledge

Language Development

1. What are two ways you can determine the meanings of new words?

2. How can previewing help you understand a text? What do you do when you preview?

3. What are two characteristics of a narrative text?

4. Do the two songs in Part 1 express the same point of view? Explain.

5. What are some sequence words? Why do you use them?

6. What is a timeline? What does a timeline show you?

7. Give an example of a sentence in the simple past. How is the verb formed?

8. What is an editing checklist?

Academic Content

1. What new social studies vocabulary did you learn in Part 1? What do the words mean?

2. What was the "Boston Tea Party"? Why was it important?

3. What was one cause of the American Revolution?

Statue of a Minute Man; Minute Men were not soldiers, but they were ready to help fight the British. ▶

Prepare to Read

OBJECTIVES
LANGUAGE DEVELOPMENT

Reading:
- Vocabulary building: *Context, dictionary skills*
- Reading strategy: *Using knowledge and experiences to predict*
- Literary element: *Compare and contrast*
- Text types: *Autobiography/ personal narrative, pamphlet*

Writing:
- Freewriting
- Journal/diary entry
- Editing checklist

Listening/Speaking:
- Culture: *Connecting experiences*
- Compare and contrast
- Venn diagram

Grammar:
- Subject-verb agreement
- Pronouns

Viewing/Representing:
- Maps, illustrations, photographs

ACADEMIC CONTENT
- Social studies vocabulary
- Chinese culture

BACKGROUND

Daughter of China is an autobiography. In an autobiography, the author uses personal narrative to tell about his or her life. In these excerpts from *Daughter of China*, the narrator describes situations in which different points of view are based on language, culture, or family background. She tells how her own point of view changes.

Make connections *Daughter of China* takes place when very few people were allowed to travel to and from China. It was sometimes dangerous for the Chinese to question authority or to break rules of the culture.

In the 1980s, the Chinese government changed some laws. It was then easier to travel to and from China. People were freer to express their opinions and act in less traditional ways.

Look at the map. Answer the questions with a partner.

1. Name one country that shares a border with China.
2. What large bodies of water border on China?

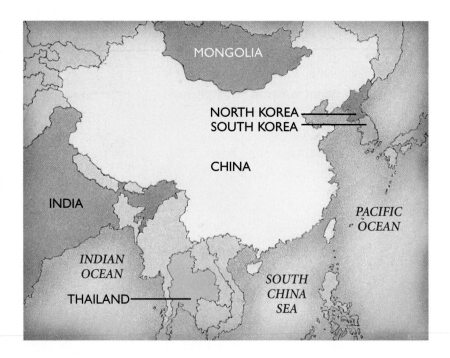

LEARN KEY WORDS

affection
customarily
dialect
scandalized
translate
witness

VOCABULARY

Read these sentences. Use the context to figure out the meaning of the **red** words. Use a dictionary to check your answers. Write each word and its meaning in your notebook.

1. In some cultures, people do not hug or kiss in front of others because they do not like to show **affection** in public.
2. We **customarily** eat dinner at 8:00, but tonight we will eat earlier.
3. He speaks in the **dialect** of Lishi, but people from other parts of China can understand him.
4. He did shocking things that upset and **scandalized** the villagers.
5. Jim asked Li to **translate** the Chinese story into English.
6. As a **witness** at her friend's wedding, Julie had to sign an official document saying that she had attended the ceremony.

READING STRATEGY

Using Knowledge and Experience to Predict

Use your own knowledge and experience to help you **predict** what is in the text. As you preview and skim the text, ask yourself:

- When and where does the story happen?
- What do I know about this time and place?
- What can I guess about the characters and their lives?
- What is my purpose for reading this text?

▲ Detail of Chinese palace roof

Personal Narrative

As you preview and skim the text, use your knowledge and experience to predict. What do you know about the places and cultures in the text? Can you guess what conflicts the characters might face? What would you do in their place?

from

Daughter of China

Meihong Xu and Larry Engelmann

In these excerpts, the narrator first talks about how point of view is shaped, or influenced, by words that exist or don't exist in a particular language. Then she tells what happened when her aunt did not follow the rules of the culture, and how people reacted to this. Next, she tells about an experience that shows differences in the points of view of Chinese students and Americans. Finally she describes ways her own point of view changed.

Chinese fan made of carved ivory ▶

He told my mother that he and Lingdi discovered that they liked each other very much. (In the dialect of Lishi there is no word for love. In place of that word, the people use the words "respect," "like," and "**cherish**." A marriage takes place between a young man and woman who "like" each other. As husband and wife they "respect" each other. Children respect their **elders**, and parents "cherish" their children. Words expressing stronger affections do not exist in our dialect. Some feelings, we believe, are too **profound** for words.) "Thank you for introducing me to her," he said. "We plan to marry next month and we would like you to be the witness at our wedding."

My mother was surprised and delighted. "Good," was all she could say. "Good." She smiled broadly when she spoke. . . .

---

cherish, care for someone lovingly
elders, older people
profound, great

I attended Lingdi's wedding. It was the first time I'd seen her in more than two years. She was smiling and laughing like a girl again. I noticed right away that she walked straight and held her head high. She was happier than I had ever seen her before.

After their honeymoon in Shanghai, Lingdi and her husband came back to the village to live there **permanently.** Her husband worked in Lingdi's garden with her and in the fields beside her, like a **peasant.** In the summer, village women customarily carried an umbrella to protect their skin from the sun. He always carried Lingdi's umbrella for her and walked beside her. Most shocking of all, they held hands when they walked in the countryside. Sometimes they even paused and Lingdi's husband kissed her on the hand or on the cheek. The other villagers were scandalized. They had never before seen this sort of **brazen** public behavior. Indeed, I had never before seen a man and woman embrace or hold hands or in any way publicly reveal romantic feelings in the village. I was **utterly** fascinated when I watched them.

Naturally, people whispered about them. There was something very different about these two. They made others uncomfortable and **jealous**.

* * *

▲ Farmers working in a rice field in China

---

permanently, forever
peasant, poor worker
brazen, bold; rude
utterly, completely
jealous, wishing you had what someone else has

BEFORE YOU GO ON . . .

1 What words are used instead of *love* in the Lishi dialect?

2 What behavior scandalized the villagers?

HOW ABOUT YOU?

• What do you think about the behavior of Lingdi and her husband? What do you think of the villagers' reaction to them?

◀ Faculty and students at the Johns Hopkins-Nanjing University Center for Chinese and American Studies, Fall, 1988; Meihong, first row, seventh from right

▲ PLA Institute of International Relations, faculty officers; Meihong, second row, far left

Meihong at the PLA Institute, summer uniform, 1987 ▶

In the summer of 1988, in order to prepare for a special program being **initiated** at the **Institute**, I was selected to study for one year at the Center for Chinese and American Studies, a two-year-old educational **joint venture** of Nanjing University and the Johns Hopkins University in the United States. The Center was located within its own walled compound **adjacent to** Nanjing University. At the Center, intended to be a model of international cooperation, Chinese and American students and **faculty** lived together in a single large complex of classrooms, apartments, offices, assembly halls and dormitory rooms as well as a library and cafeteria. The Chinese students sent to the Center were customarily mid-career professionals—government **bureaucrats**, **Party officials**, junior university professors, military officers, journalists or administrators—who had

---

initiated, started; began
Institute, Chinese military training school, located in Nanjing
joint venture, project undertaken by two universities
adjacent to, next to

faculty, teachers and instructors
bureaucrats, officials; important people
Party officials, officials of the Communist Party

Meihong with her mother, 1987 ▶

Meihong and her family, 1990, just before she departed from China; Mother and father, first row; Meihong, second row, second from right ▼

Meihong at work, PLA Institute ▶

been out of school several years and were chosen by their work units to have a chance to study English and other academic subjects (history, political science, economics, international relations) with a small group of **distinguished** visiting American instructors.

American students at the Center were almost all young graduate students from American universities, but also included a few American military officers who came to the Center to study Chinese language and history with selected Chinese instructors. . . .

---

distinguished, famous and respected by many people

BEFORE YOU GO ON . . .

1 What was the Center for Chinese and American studies?
2 What was the purpose of the Center?

HOW ABOUT YOU?

● Would you like to attend a center like this? Why or why not?

For the first time in my life I came into close contact with American students and professors who spoke freely about politics and cultural values, who joked openly about their own political and cultural values, who joked openly about their own political leaders, who were unafraid of **retribution**, who had great hopes and few fears for either the present or the future. The first time one of the American professors told a **disparagingly** humorous story about one of America's **Founding Fathers**, we were **stunned**. We could not understand how he dared to say such things. After showing us a copy of a famous painting of General George Washington crossing the Delaware River, he asked us

LITERARY ELEMENT

Comparing and contrasting is one way authors can express an important idea. For example, to show how a character develops, an author might compare and contrast the character's new attitude toward something with a previous attitude that he or she has outgrown.

▲ *Washington Crossing the Delaware* by Emanuel Gottlieb Leutze, 1851

why we thought General Washington stood up in the boat. The students spent several minutes guessing. When they finally asked for the "correct" answer, the professor told us, "Because he knew if he sat down, someone would hand him an oar." The students were dead silent. The professor said it was a joke. "Maybe it just doesn't translate well," he said, and continued on with his lecture.

The Americans were a curious group and we Chinese students talked constantly about them. Participating day after day in discussions at the Center, reading and **socializing** with these Americans, I felt something inside myself coming loose. I began to laugh at some of the **absurdities** of the world and the people around me and lost my sense of **awe** of people in power. I felt I was finding myself—my own identity. I began to think **critically** and independently. Like all Chinese students, I'd always mistaken memorization for education. I thought there was one truth and one way and one system that was best for all people and that I was part of it. Now nothing was as simple as it once was.

---

socializing, spending time with other people
absurdities, things that are extremely silly
awe, great wonder
critically, looking for faults

About the Authors

Meihong Xu and Larry Engelmann

Meihong Xu was born in China into a peasant family. She dreamed of being an officer in the People's Liberation Army. Larry Engelmann was her professor. Eventually she became disillusioned with the Chinese government. She left China and now lives in California.

BEFORE YOU GO ON . . .

1 Why didn't the students laugh at the professor's joke?

2 What are some ways the narrator's thinking changed as a result of her experience with the Americans?

HOW ABOUT YOU?

- Have you ever found it difficult to understand a joke in another culture? Explain.

Review and Practice

What did you learn about Chinese culture from reading the excerpts from *Daughter of China*? Reread the text. Then copy this word web into your notebook. On the branches of the web, write facts that you learned about Chinese culture and language.

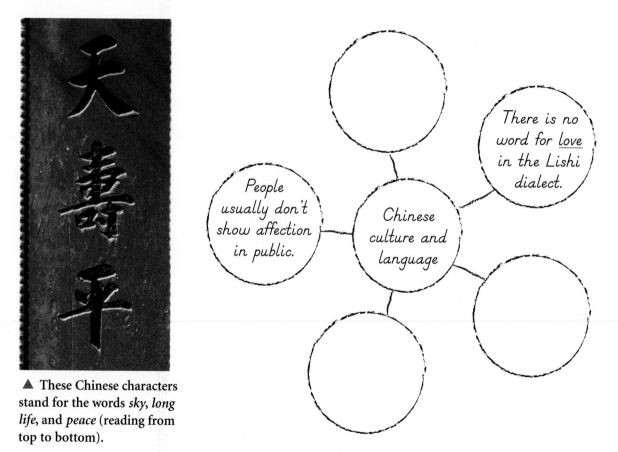

▲ These Chinese characters stand for the words *sky, long life,* and *peace* (reading from top to bottom).

Work in a small group. Compare your word webs. Use information from all of your webs to create a web for your group. Take turns using the web to say things about Chinese culture. Share your group word web with the class.

EXTENSION

Look again at the word web that your group made. How is the Chinese culture described in the web different from U.S. culture? How is it the same? Copy the Venn diagram into your notebook. Use it to compare and contrast U.S. culture and Chinese culture as described in the text.

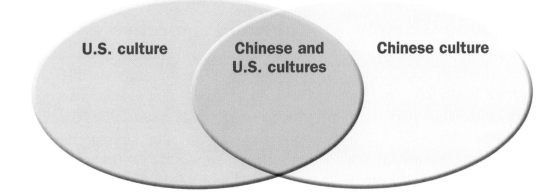

U.S. culture

Chinese and U.S. cultures

Chinese culture

DISCUSSION

Discuss in pairs or small groups.

1. Why is there no word for *love* in the Lishi dialect? What words do people use?
2. What do you think the Chinese and American university students learned from each other?
3. How did the narrator's point of view change after her contact with the Americans at the Center?
4. In the excerpts from *Daughter of China*, the narrator describes behavior that is either appropriate or inappropriate, depending on point of view. Identify one of these descriptions and discuss it.

This is an informational pamphlet that suggests ways in which people can be more respectful of cultural differences. Pamphlets like this are nonfiction. Look at the illustrations. Who do you think this pamphlet is for?

Understanding Cultural Differences

Sandy Cameron

Welcome to Camp Gateway

Welcome to another fun-filled summer at Camp Gateway. As you all know, Camp Gateway prides itself on attracting and bringing together campers and staff members from **diverse** cultural backgrounds. The unique opportunity our camp provides its campers and staff can be wonderfully rewarding, but it requires a spirit of trust, patience, and cooperation from every one of us. This pamphlet suggests a variety of ways in which we can be more respectful of our cultural differences and less likely to **offend** our fellow campers and staff members.

diverse, different; completely unalike
offend, make someone angry or upset

Cultural Perspective

Being sensitive to cultural differences often helps us avoid misunderstandings. For example, think about the many ways in which a simple smile might be interpreted, depending on one's cultural **perspective**. For someone born in the United States, a smile would probably be understood to show pleasure or happiness. In Japan, too, people smile when they are happy. But Japanese people also smile when they are confused or embarrassed. In some other Asian cultures, people smile to show disagreement, anger, and frustration. Some people from Asia will not smile for official

perspective, point of view

32

photos, such as passport photos, because these are considered serious occasions. They want to appear to be taking the situation seriously.

Whether to **establish eye contact** varies around the world as well. People from many Asian and Latin American cultures avoid direct eye contact because looking directly at someone can seem disrespectful. An American person might think exactly the opposite—that it is disrespectful not to look someone in the eye. So think twice before you judge someone for meeting or not meeting your glance.

Overcoming Language Barriers

Language differences can make communication difficult, but you can do things to help get your point across. Talk slowly and clearly. It may sound obvious, but don't shout at people if they don't understand what you are saying. Say what you want to say in a different way or repeat your words more slowly. Use other methods of communication, such as making drawings or acting out your ideas.

When speaking, avoid using slang expressions. Slang is more difficult for someone who is not a native speaker of your language. Instead, use more formal language.

---

establish eye contact, look at someone directly in the eyes

In many cultures, people have difficulty saying "no" to a request, and some people may say "yes" when their answer is really "no." To be respectful of this fact, phrase questions so that they do not require a yes-or-no answer. A question such as "Would you rather play tennis or shoot archery?" is easier for many people to answer truthfully than "Would you like to play tennis?"

BEFORE YOU GO ON . . .

1 In some Asian cultures, what emotions other than happiness can be shown by a smile?

2 Explain how eye contact varies from culture to culture.

HOW ABOUT YOU?

• How do you feel about the illustrations on these pages? What effect do they have on you?

Names and Time

People in the United States generally call others by their first names very soon after meeting them, but this is not true in all cultures. It's important to know what a person from another country prefers to be called. You should let others know what name they should call you. If necessary, pronounce each other's names slowly or write them down for each other.

Cultural backgrounds often dictate what people expect with regard to time and **punctuality**. What you consider to be on time, late, and early might be different from your fellow campers' and staff members' ideas. Don't be afraid to ask someone to **clarify** exactly when he or she expects you to be somewhere.

Learning about other cultures and being respectful of differences can **go a long way toward** ensuring that every camper and staff member has a rewarding and memorable experience here at Camp Gateway.

---

punctuality, being on time
clarify, explain or make clear
go a long way toward, do a lot to; help to

Practice begins at 2:15. Don't be late.

BEFORE YOU GO ON . . .

1. Why is it important to find out what name a person prefers to be called?

2. Why might a person from another culture have ideas about time and lateness that are different from yours?

HOW ABOUT YOU?

- What other advice do you have for getting along well with people from other cultures?

Link the Readings

Think about the texts you read in this part as you look at the chart. Then copy the chart into your notebook and complete it.

Title of Selection	Genre	Fiction or Nonfiction	Purpose of Selection	Different Points of View
From *Daughter of China*	autobiography/ personal narrative			
"Understanding Cultural Differences"				attitudes about eye contact

DISCUSSION

Discuss in pairs or small groups.

1. Both of the texts in Part 2 tell how people from different cultures can have different points of view. How does awareness of these points of view help people from different cultures get along better?
2. If you could talk with the professor you read about in *Daughter of China*, what advice would you give him about communicating with the students?
3. How did you use knowledge and experience to predict in Part 2?

Connect to Writing

GRAMMAR

Subject-Verb Agreement in the Simple Present

When you use the simple present, the subject and verb must "agree." This means that when you use *he/she* or *it*, the verb must end in **-s.**

Subject	Verb
I We They	**speak** freely about my political ideas. **attend** the wedding. **work** like a machine.
He She It	**speaks** freely about politics. **attends** the wedding. **works** well.

Practice

Write the sentences in your notebook. Use the correct verb.

1. In summer, they (carry / carries) umbrellas to protect their skin from the sun.
2. Lingdi's husband (kiss / kisses) her on the hand or on the cheek.
3. The professor (tell / tells) the students funny jokes.

Write the sentences in your notebook. Use the correct subject.

1. (A marriage / Marriages) takes place between a young man and woman who "like" each other.
2. (A child / Children) respect their elders.
3. (Students / A student) live in a single large complex.

SKILLS FOR WRITING

Writing Journal Entries to Develop Fluency

A journal or diary is a collection of writings about your experiences, thoughts, and feelings.

Each separate writing in a journal or diary is called an entry. Journal or diary entries are usually informal—you can make notes rather than write in complete sentences. With regular practice, this kind of writing can help you express your ideas more quickly and easily.

Read the journal entry. Then answer the questions.

Kevin D. Ascher

October 13

I almost always eat healthy foods, both at home and at school. As I ate my lunch at school today, some of the people sitting at my table teased me about what I was eating. This made me extremely mad because they were making fun of my personal beliefs. I have many good reasons to eat good foods.

First of all, nutritious foods taste good. Second, I want to live a long and healthy life. Last, but not least, I stand up for what I think is right, even if there is no one standing there with me. I hope all those who don't eat good foods try them and give them a chance.

1. What is this journal entry about?
2. What do you know about the writer from this journal entry?
3. Do you think the journal entry is interesting? Why or why not?

WRITING ASSIGNMENT

Journal Entry

You will write a journal entry describing a situation in which your point of view was different from that of others.

1. **Read** Reread the first excerpt from *Daughter of China.* When Meihong Xu sees the behavior of Lingdi and her husband, she reacts differently from the way the other villagers do. Why?

Writing Strategy: Freewriting

Sometimes it is useful to time yourself when you freewrite. Set a timer for five minutes and begin writing. Write as fast as you can about the topic you have chosen. Do not worry about correct grammar or spelling or punctuation. The page below is an example of freewriting. The writer is exploring the way she feels about Lingdi and her husband.

> Lingdi and her husband are just people in love. I think it's so sweet. They show their affection. They don't care what people think. Maybe they should care. When some people see them holding hands, they are scandalized. I'm not—I think it's great. It makes me feel like I hope I'm like that when I'm older.

---

2. **Freewrite your journal entry** Take out a clean piece of paper, set a timer for five minutes, and write without stopping. Describe a situation in which your point of view was different from that of others. How was your reaction to the situation different? How did you feel?

EDITING CHECKLIST

Did you . . .

▶ describe the situation?

▶ give details about the differences between your point of view and that of the other person(s)?

▶ tell how you felt?

Check Your Knowledge

Language Development

1. Describe how you use knowledge and experience to predict what is in a text.

2. What genre is *Daughter of China*? What are some characteristics of this genre?

3. What graphic organizer is helpful for comparing and contrasting? Why?

4. What is subject-verb agreement? Give an example.

5. Describe freewriting. When can you use freewriting?

Academic Content

1. What new social studies vocabulary did you learn in Part 2? What do the words mean?

2. What did you learn about Chinese culture in the excerpts from *Daughter of China*?

3. Describe some of the cultural differences you learned about in Part 2.

Put It All Together

OBJECTIVES

Integrate Skills
- Listening/
  Speaking:
  Presentation
- Writing:
  *Personal
  narrative*

**Investigate
Themes**
- Projects
- Further
  reading

PERSONAL NARRATIVE

In a personal narrative, you tell a story about events or people in your life. The story is about your personal experience. To convey your experience, be sure to describe your feelings and reactions to a conflict or problem.

You will organize and present an oral personal narrative.

 Think about it Think about some good and bad experiences you have had. Make a list of them. Then read your lists and choose an experience for your narrative.

2 Organize Your narrative should have a beginning, a middle, and an end. Make a list of the events that occur in your narrative. Then write each event on a card. Organize your cards in the order that the events happened. On the card that tells the conflict, write *conflict*. Write a sequence word in the top left corner of each card, as appropriate.

Work with a partner. Read each other's cards and ask questions. Then add interesting details to your cards.

 Practice Using your cards, practice telling your story. Practice several times, then put the cards away. Tell your story again from memory.

4 Present and evaluate Work in small groups. Present your story to the group without using your cards. After each group member finishes, evaluate the presentation. What did you like best about the presentation? Do you have suggestions for improvement?

SPEAKING TIPS

- Speak naturally and with feeling.
- Make eye contact with your audience as you speak.

LISTENING TIPS

- Look at the speaker as he or she speaks.
- Do not interrupt the speaker. Save your questions until the speaker is finished.

PERSONAL NARRATIVE

A written personal narrative includes the following characteristics:

- a first-person narrator—or "I"—that tells the story
- a clear sequence of events telling the beginning, the middle, and the end
- the narrator's feelings and reactions to a conflict, problem, or situation
- a conclusion that tells how the conflict or situation is resolved

You will write a personal narrative describing an experience in which your point of view was different from that of people around you. Use the steps above and the model essay to help you.

1 **Prewrite** Think about a situation in which you reacted differently from other people. Be sure that the different points of view in the situation will be clear to your reader. Use a chart to list the events that you will write about in your personal narrative. Then write sequence words in front of your events to help your readers follow the order of events.

WRITING TIP

One way to show the different points of view clearly in your narrative is to compare and contrast them. For example, in one paragraph, you can describe your point of view. In another paragraph, you can describe the other point of view.

Before you write a first draft of your personal narrative, read the following student model. Notice the characteristics of a personal narrative.

Lauren Younkins

Two Views of a Mouse

Yesterday, in science class, something happened that everyone thought was funny—except me.

In one corner of the classroom, we have a snake and a mouse, which we observe and study. The class was observing the snake and learning about its habitat. Then suddenly Billy said that the mouse wasn't in its cage! No one knew where it was.

I was so frightened that I jumped right up on my desk! I must have looked pretty silly because the other students looked at me and laughed. I couldn't believe that they weren't frightened at all!

Then Meredith found the mouse, picked it up, and put it back in its cage. Finally, everything calmed down, and we continued learning.

The writer introduces the situation in an interesting way to get readers' attention.

She adds details to build excitement.

The writer contrasts her point of view with that of the other students.

Her conclusion tells how the situation was resolved.

2 **Draft** Use the model and your chart to write your personal narrative.

- Start your narrative in an exciting way, so readers will be interested in your story. For example, briefly describe the characters and introduce your conflict or situation. Notice how the student starts her narrative. How does she get you interested in her story?

- Give more details about the conflict or situation in the next paragraph. Try to build excitement or suspense about the events.

- Clearly explain or contrast the different points of view. Tell how you felt about the situation and how the other people felt.

- Conclude your narrative by describing how the conflict or situation was resolved. If appropriate, explain what you learned from this experience.

3 **Edit** Work in pairs. Trade papers and read each other's narratives. Use the questions in the editing checklist to evaluate each other's work.

EDITING CHECKLIST

Did you . . .

▶ write about events in the order that they happened?

▶ use sequence words to make the order of events clear?

▶ check to make sure all the subjects and verbs agree?

4 **Revise** Revise your personal narrative. Add details and correct mistakes, if necessary.

5 **Publish** Share your narrative with your teacher and classmates.

PROJECTS

Work in pairs or small groups. Choose one of these projects.

1 With a family member, make a list of customs that your family follows. Copy the list onto a poster or overhead transparency. Then present your family customs to the class. Include details. If possible, bring photographs or objects to illustrate your presentation.

2 Create a magazine ad for your school. Show or tell how people can learn to work and cooperate with others. Display your ad.

3 Use the Internet to find out more about the American Revolution and the Boston Tea Party. Make a list of facts. Then make a poster about the Revolution. You might want to include a timeline or a map showing places where major events happened.

4 Go to the library or use the Internet to find the poem *Paul Revere's Ride* by Henry Wadsworth Longfellow. Make a book with a copy of the poem and an illustration. Read the poem to your class and show your book.

5 Find recordings of some songs from the American colonial period. Share the recordings with your class.

Further Reading

To find out more about the theme of this unit, choose from these reading suggestions.

The Prince and the Pauper, **Mark Twain** In sixteenth-century England, two boys are born on the same day and grow up looking alike. One is Tom Canty, a beggar; the other is Edward, a prince. The boys meet by accident and decide to trade clothes just for fun. As a result, people treat Canty like a prince and Edward like a beggar.

George Washington: Soldier, Hero, and President, **Justine and Ron Fontes** This biography tells the story of Washington's childhood, his life as a farmer, his role in the American Revolution, and his years as the first president of the United States. Throughout, we come to understand Washington's ideals and how they were formed.

A White Heron and other American Short Stories, **Sarah Orne Jewett and others** A young man is friendly to Sylvia, and Sylvia wants him to like her. The man is a hunter in search of a white heron. Sylvia knows where the heron's nest is, but should she tell him? Sylvia can't decide what is more important—protecting this beautiful bird or making a new friend. Her point of view changes several times as she decides.

Homesick: My Own Story, **Jean Fritz** This blend of fact and fiction is based on the author's childhood in China during the 1920s. She loved many things about life in China. But her parents' stories of home in America made her feel homesick for a place she had never seen.

Give Me Liberty: The Story of the Declaration of Independence, **Russell Freedman** Russell Freedman takes us back to the days before, during, and after the American Revolution. We get to know people like Thomas Jefferson, whose views helped shape a new nation. We also come to understand the significance of the Declaration of Independence, both then and now.

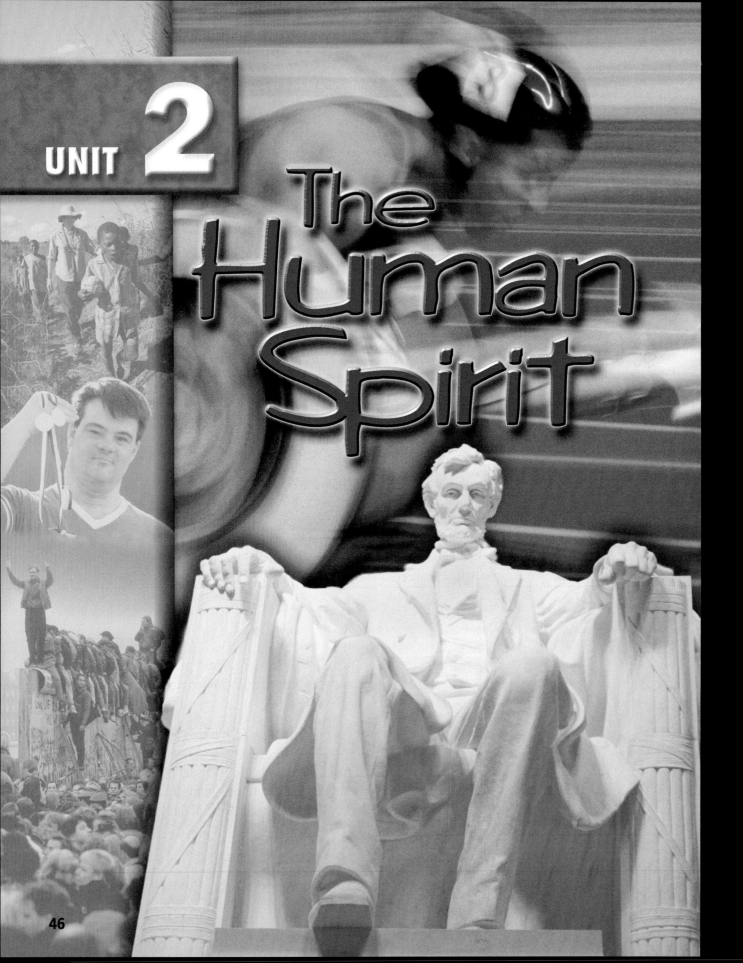

UNIT 2

The Human Spirit

PART 1

- "Abraham Lincoln"
- "Nancy Hanks," Rosemary Carr and Stephen Vincent Benét
- "Lincoln," John Gould Fletcher

PART 2

- *Sor Juana Inés de la Cruz,* Kathleen Thompson
- "The Peace Corps"

For some people, the human spirit is the courage to stand up for what they believe. For other people, it is the desire to use their talents and to live a life of service. For still others, it is the ability to succeed even after repeated failures. In this unit, you will read about people who have these qualities.

In Part 1, you will read a biographical article and two poems about Abraham Lincoln, a man who experienced sadness and failure, but who went on to demonstrate what the human spirit can accomplish. As president of the United States, he successfully led the country through one of the most difficult periods in its history—the Civil War.

In Part 2, you will learn about Sor Juana Inés de la Cruz, a Mexican woman who overcame difficulties to live a life of creativity, intelligence, honesty, and courage. You will also read about the Peace Corps, an organization that helps people all over the world in many ways.

Prepare to Read

OBJECTIVES

LANGUAGE DEVELOPMENT

Reading:
- Vocabulary building: *Context, dictionary skills*
- Reading strategy: *Taking notes*
- Text types: *Biographical article, poetry*
- Literary elements: *Rhyme, simile*
- Graphic organizers: *Timeline, chart*

Writing:
- Word web
- Opinion statements/ persuasive paragraph
- Self-evaluation
- Editing checklist

Listening/Speaking:
- Persuasion/opinion
- Group decision-making

Grammar:
- Real conditionals
- Mechanics

Viewing/Representing:
- Maps, photographs, illustrations

ACADEMIC CONTENT

- Social studies vocabulary
- Abraham Lincoln
- Slavery and the Civil War

BACKGROUND

"Abraham Lincoln" is a biographical article about President Lincoln, who led the country through a difficult period—the American Civil War (1861–1865).

Make connections Abraham Lincoln was elected president on November 6, 1860. At this time, the United States was made up of "free states" (mainly in the North) and "slave states" (mainly in the South). The North was an industrial society where many people worked in factories. The South was a farming society that depended on slave labor. In 1860, fearing restrictions on slavery, seven southern states seceded—or broke away—from the United States. By 1861, four more southern states seceded. These states called themselves the Confederacy. The other states remained loyal to the United States. These states were known as the Union.

Look at the map and answer the questions.

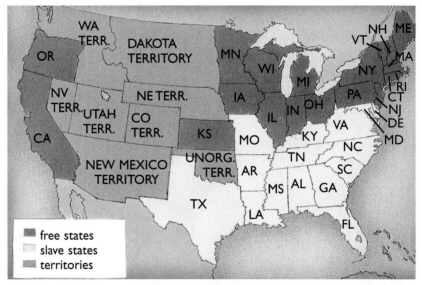

- free states
- slave states
- territories

1. How many states and territories were there in 1861?
2. Which states were "free states"?
3. Which states were "slave states"?

LEARN KEY WORDS

abolitionists
expansion
hardship
losses
refused
took a stand
unity

VOCABULARY

Read these sentences. Use the context to figure out the meaning of the **red** words. Use a dictionary to check your answers. Write each word and its meaning in your notebook.

1. The **abolitionists** wanted to abolish, or end, slavery.
2. Lincoln did not support the **expansion** of slavery to the new states.
3. The **hardship** of being poor and uneducated did not stop Lincoln.
4. Lincoln experienced many **losses**, including the death of his son.
5. Lincoln fell in love with a woman, but she **refused** to marry him.
6. Lincoln **took a stand** against the spread of slavery to new states.
7. After the war, Lincoln wanted to bring **unity** back to the divided country.

READING STRATEGY

Taking Notes

Taking notes as you read can help you focus your attention and remember facts more easily. To takes notes, you have to keep in mind your purpose for reading the text.

When you take notes, don't write complete sentences. Use abbreviations when possible. For example:

- born Feb. 12, 1809, in KY
- attended school less than one year

You can use your notes later to help you write about the text or study for a test.

Social Studies

Abraham Lincoln became president of the United States in 1860, just before the Civil War began. As you read about Lincoln, take notes. What is your purpose for reading this text? If it is to learn about Abraham Lincoln and U.S. history, include names, dates, and important events in Lincoln's life.

Abraham Lincoln

Abraham Lincoln **knew** hardship, sadness, and disappointment. He was born on February 12, 1809, on a farm in Kentucky. The house where he was born was a one-room cabin with a dirt floor. His father, Thomas Lincoln, never received any **formal education**. He worked as a carpenter and farmer. His mother, Nancy Hanks Lincoln, came from a poor Virginia family. She never went to school, and she never learned to write. During his whole life, Lincoln

◄ President Lincoln

---

knew, was familiar with; experienced
formal education, learning in a school

attended less than one year of school. His younger brother, Thomas, died in **infancy**. His mother died when he was nine years old.

As an adult, Lincoln faced other losses. His sister died in childbirth. Three of his sons died young. Lincoln lost jobs and elections. Yet, this man went on to become president of the United States and to lead the country through one of the most difficult periods of its history.

Lincoln's Education

Although Lincoln did not have much formal education, he loved to read. As a child, he borrowed books from his neighbors. One book that was very important to him was *The Life of Washington* by Parson Mason Weems. He read books on a wide variety of subjects, including law, and eventually he became a lawyer and a **politician**.

---

infancy, the time when a person is a baby
politician, a person who works in the government or politics

BEFORE YOU GO ON . . .

1. When was Abraham Lincoln born? Where?
2. What were some of the hardships Lincoln faced when he was young?

HOW ABOUT YOU?
- How is Lincoln's early life like your own? How is Lincoln's life different from yours?

◀ The cabin where Lincoln was born

Early Political Career

In 1832, Lincoln **ran for** a seat in the Illinois House of Representatives. He lost. In 1834, he ran again. This time he won. He won again in 1836, 1838, and 1840. In 1837, for the first time, Lincoln took a public stand against slavery. He believed slavery was wrong, and he was against the spread of slavery into new states.

In 1837, Lincoln asked a woman named Mary Owens to marry him, but she refused. In 1839, Lincoln met Mary Ann Todd. Lincoln married Mary Todd in 1842. They had four sons, but only one of them, Robert Todd Lincoln, lived to be an adult. Edward, William, and Thomas all died before they were twenty years old.

---

ran for, tried to get elected

Lincoln's wife,
Mary Todd Lincoln ▶

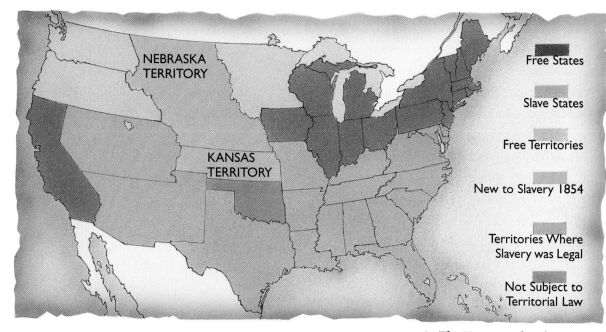

NEBRASKA TERRITORY

KANSAS TERRITORY

Free States

Slave States

Free Territories

New to Slavery 1854

Territories Where Slavery was Legal

Not Subject to Territorial Law

▲ The Kansas-Nebraska Act stated that voters in Kansas and Nebraska could decide whether they would allow slavery in their territory.

The Issue of Slavery

Cotton growing became a big business in the southern United States. As more people began to grow cotton, more slaves were needed to work on the **plantations**.

In 1849, Lincoln returned to his law **practice**. In 1854, Congress passed the Kansas-Nebraska Act. This act created the territories of Kansas and Nebraska. It also stated that if the territories applied to become states, the voters in these territories could decide whether or not slavery would be allowed.

Until then, slavery had been allowed only in slave states identified in the Missouri Compromise of 1820. Many people, who called themselves abolitionists, wanted to end slavery everywhere. Lincoln believed that slavery was wrong. However, he was not an abolitionist; he did not want to make slavery illegal in states where it already existed. He wanted to stop the expansion of slavery into new territories. So, once again, he entered political life.

---

plantations, large farms in the South
practice, the work of a doctor or lawyer (a medical practice, a law practice)

BEFORE YOU GO ON . . .

1 What happened the first time that Lincoln ran for election? What happened the second time?

2 What stand did Lincoln take on slavery?

HOW ABOUT YOU?

• Did you ever try to do something and fail, and then try it later and succeed? Describe the experience.

The Race against Douglas

The country continued to be divided on the issue of slavery. In the 1857 *Dred Scott* decision, the United States Supreme Court ruled that Congress could not prohibit slavery in the territories. In 1858, Illinois Senator Stephen Douglas, who believed that new territories should make their own decisions about slavery, ran for re-election to the Senate. The Republican Party chose Lincoln to run against him. Lincoln and Douglas had several **debates**. These debates with Douglas brought Lincoln national attention. Lincoln lost the election, but now the country knew him. Finally, in 1860, Abraham Lincoln was elected sixteenth president of the United States.

▲ Slaves working in the cotton fields

The Civil War

In 1861, the southern states **seceded** and formed the Confederacy. The Civil War started when Confederate soldiers attacked Fort Sumter in Charleston, South Carolina. Lincoln raised a volunteer army to fight against them. He led the country through four long, terrible years of civil war. In 1863, he issued the Emancipation Proclamation, which freed the slaves in the Confederate states. He also delivered the Gettysburg Address, one of the most famous speeches in American history.

---

debates, public talks at which people discuss different opinions about an issue
seceded, formally stopped being part of a country

▲ Attack on Fort Sumter

Efforts to Reunify the Country

The Gettysburg Address was made more than a year before the end of the Civil War, but in this speech Lincoln spoke about healing and unity for the whole country. He **dedicated** the Gettysburg battlefield to all the soldiers who had died there. After the war ended, Lincoln called on the country to support the South through the period of **Reconstruction**. It was most important to him to reunite the North and the South.

Abraham Lincoln also made Thanksgiving a national holiday. The first national Thanksgiving holiday was observed on November 26, 1863.

On March 4, 1865, Lincoln was elected president for a second term.

▲ Artist's depiction of Lincoln's assassination

Lincoln's Assassination

On April 14, 1865, President Lincoln was assassinated. He was shot in the evening while he was watching a play at Ford's Theatre in Washington, D.C. He died the next morning. The man who killed him was named John Wilkes Booth. Lincoln was fifty-six years old at the time of his death. On April 15, Andrew Johnson, Lincoln's vice president, took the office of the president. Lincoln's body was taken back to Illinois to be buried at Oak Ridge Cemetery in Springfield.

After Lincoln's death, Secretary of War Edwin M. Stanton recognized the great spirit of this man when he said, "Now he belongs to **the ages**."

---

dedicated, set apart for a purpose
Reconstruction, the rebuilding after the Civil War
the ages, all of time and human history

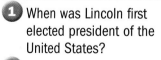

BEFORE YOU GO ON . . .

1 When was Lincoln first elected president of the United States?

2 In what speech did Lincoln talk about unity?

HOW ABOUT YOU?

• Do you think Lincoln was a great leader? Why or why not?

Review and Practice

Reread the text and look at the notes you took. Organize your notes using each of these graphic organizers.

Timeline: Copy the timeline into your notebook. Use your notes to complete it by writing important events in Lincoln's life near the appropriate dates.

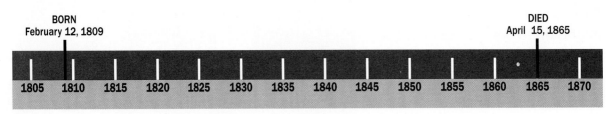

BORN
February 12, 1809

DIED
April 15, 1865

1805   1810   1815   1820   1825   1830   1835   1840   1845   1850   1855   1860   1865   1870

Chart: Copy the chart into your notebook. Use your notes to complete each column with important events in Lincoln's life. Use dates when you can.

Early Life	Early Political Career	Presidency
1809: Lincoln is born.		

Do your two graphic organizers give you the same information or different information? Which one is more complete? Which one would be better to study from? Choose one of the graphic organizers and use it to help you tell a partner about Lincoln's life.

EXTENSION

Work in groups. Imagine that it is 1859 and Abraham Lincoln is running for president. You are trying to persuade your friends to vote for him. Talk about three or more reasons why Lincoln would be a good president. Support your reasons with facts from his life.

DISCUSSION

Discuss in pairs or small groups.

1. How did Lincoln's love of reading help prepare him to become a leader?
2. Summarize Lincoln's political career. What successes did he have? What failures?
3. What do you admire most about Lincoln? Why?

◀ An election banner showing Lincoln and Hamlin (vice president during Lincoln's first term)

Poetry

This is a poem about Abraham Lincoln's mother, Nancy Hanks. The poem is in four stanzas, or groups of lines. The last stanza contains questions the poet imagines Nancy Hanks might ask about her son. How would you answer her questions?

Nancy Hanks

If Nancy Hanks
Came back as a **ghost**,
Seeking news
Of what she loved most,
She'd ask first
"Where's my son?
What's happened to Abe?
What's he done?

"Poor little Abe
Left all alone
Except for Tom
Who's a **rolling stone**:
He was only nine
The year I died,
I remember still
How hard he cried.

"**Scraping along**
In a little **shack**,
With hardly a shirt
To cover his back,
And a **prairie** wind
To blow him down,
Or **pinching times**
If he went to town.

"You wouldn't know
About my son?
Did he grow tall?
Did he have fun?
Did he learn to read?
Did he get to town?
Do you know his name?
Did he **get on**?"

**Rosemary Carr and
Stephen Vincent Benét**

---

ghost, the spirit of a dead
   person
rolling stone, someone who
   doesn't stay in one place for
   very long; someone who
   wanders around

---

scraping along, trying to survive
   without much money
shack, a very small, poorly built
   house, usually one room
prairie, a big field covered with
   wild grass and flowers
pinching times, a time when
   you have very little money or
   food
get on, do well

LITERARY ELEMENT

Words that *rhyme* have the same final sound. In the poem "Nancy Hanks," many of the words rhyme—for example, *ghost* and *most*. Can you find other examples of rhyme?

BEFORE YOU GO ON . . .

1. What is the first question Nancy Hanks would ask if she came back as a ghost?
2. *Alone* and *stone* rhyme. Name two other words from the poem that rhyme.

HOW ABOUT YOU?

- How do you feel about the poem? Explain.

As you read this poem, notice which words and phrases help you to picture Lincoln in your mind.

Lincoln

Like a **gaunt**, **scraggly** pine
Which lifts its head above the **mournful**
    sandhills;
And patiently, through dull years of
    bitter silence,
Untended and uncared for, starts to grow.

Ungainly, **laboring**, huge,
The wind of the north has twisted and
    gnarled its branches;
Yet in the heat of mid-summer days,
    when thunder clouds ring the horizon,
A nation of men shall rest beneath its shade.

And it shall protect them all,
Hold everyone safe there, watching **aloof**
    in silence;
Until at last, one **mad stray bolt** from the
    zenith
Shall strike it in an instant down to earth.

John Gould Fletcher

---

gaunt, very thin and bony
scraggly, rough; irregular
mournful, very sad
ungainly, awkward; clumsy
laboring, working very hard
aloof, away from or distant from
mad stray bolt, an unexpected flash
   of lightning
zenith, the sky; the highest point

LITERARY ELEMENT

A *simile* uses the word *like* or *as* in a comparison of two things. Similes can make descriptions more interesting. The simile in this poem compares Lincoln with a pine tree.

BEFORE YOU GO ON . . .

1. How is Lincoln like a pine tree in the poem?
2. What happens to the tree in stanza 3? How is this like what happened to Lincoln in real life?

HOW ABOUT YOU?

- Do you think this poem describes Lincoln well? Why or why not?

About the Author

John Gould Fletcher

John Gould Fletcher (1886–1950) was born in Little Rock, Arkansas. He went to Harvard University, but he quit school when his father died. He traveled to Europe and became a poet. He lived in London and knew other famous poets of the time.

Link the Readings

In Part 1, you read three texts about Abraham Lincoln. Reread the poems and look at the biographical article. Copy the chart into your notebook and complete it.

Title of Selection	Genre	Purpose of Selection	Sentence about Text
"Abraham Lincoln"			
"Nancy Hanks"			
"Lincoln"			*This poem compares Lincoln with a tall tree.*

DISCUSSION

Discuss in pairs or small groups.

1. Think about the state you are living in. Was it a state during the time Lincoln was president? When did it become a state?

2. Compare the descriptions of Lincoln's childhood in the article "Abraham Lincoln" and the poem "Nancy Hanks."

3. What makes Abraham Lincoln's life a good example of the human spirit? Can you think of another leader in the United States or in another country whose life also provides a good example of the human spirit?

Connect to Writing

GRAMMAR

Using Real Conditionals: Sentences with *if* Clauses

Real conditional sentences include a main clause and an *if* clause. The *if* clause states a condition. The main clause states the result (or possible result) of that condition.

if clause	main clause
If we win the state championship,	we will go on to the national play-offs.

main clause	*if* clause
We'll have an extra day of school in June	if school is closed for bad weather.

Notice that the *if* clause can go before or after the main clause. Use a comma when the *if* clause is before the main clause.

For a condition that *usually* happens, use the **simple present** in both clauses.

if clause	main clause
If it **rains**,	the tennis team **practices** indoors.

For a condition that *might happen in the future*, use the **simple future** in the main clause, but use the **simple present** in the *if* clause.

if clause	main clause
If my cousins **visit** this summer,	I **will take** them to the beach.

Practice

Copy the phrases into your notebook. Complete them, using the appropriate verb forms. Then compare your sentences in pairs.

1. If you study hard for the test, . . .
2. If I don't have to study tonight, . . .
3. My mother will be mad if . . .
4. If you want a copy of my notes, . . .
5. If you don't feel better tomorrow, . . .
6. Our class will go on a trip if . . .

SKILLS FOR WRITING

Persuasive Writing

When you write to persuade, you must think about who you are trying to persuade. Use arguments that are important to your readers. Consider your readers when you use pronouns such as "we" and "they."

Read the model and answer the questions.

Jeremy Ng

I believe we should study foreign languages in school. If we don't study foreign languages, businesses will suffer. Trading with other countries will be difficult. If we don't study foreign languages, we will not be able to speak with people who don't understand English. And we won't be able to deeply understand another culture. I think a foreign language should be required for all middle school and high school students.

1. Who is the writer trying to persuade?
2. What is the writer's opinion?
3. How does the writer support his opinion?

WRITING ASSIGNMENT

Persuasive Paragraph

You will write a persuasive paragraph about one of these topics:

Should schools have dress codes?
Should teenagers have credit cards?
Should grade school children have cell phones?
Should students be required to take gym class?

1. **Read** Reread the model on page 63. How does the writer try to persuade his readers?

Writing Strategy: Word Web

You can use a word web to organize your ideas for a persuasive paragraph. First write your opinion in a circle in the center. Then write reasons that support your opinion in circles around it.

Look at the word web the writer used to write the paragraph on page 63.

helps us understand other cultures

good for businesses

We should study foreign languages.

allows us to communicate with people from other countries

helpful for international trade

---

2. **Make a word web** Draw a word web in your notebook.

3. **Write a paragraph** Use your word web to write a persuasive paragraph.

EDITING CHECKLIST

Did you . . .

▶ include a topic sentence?

▶ state reasons that support your opinion?

▶ use real conditionals correctly?

64

Language Development

1. Describe the reading strategy of taking notes. How can this help you in your reading?

2. What is a biographical text?

3. What graphic organizer(s) are helpful for recording information from a social studies text?

4. What is rhyme? Give an example of two words that rhyme.

5. What is a simile? Give an example.

6. What is a real conditional? Give an example of a sentence with an *if* clause and a real conditional.

Academic Content

1. What social studies vocabulary did you learn in Part 1? What do the words mean?

2. Who was Abraham Lincoln?

3. What was the Missouri Compromise?

4. What do you know about the U.S. Civil War?

PART 2 Prepare to Read

OBJECTIVES

LANGUAGE DEVELOPMENT

Reading:
- Vocabulary building: *Context, dictionary skills*
- Reading strategies: *Making inferences, noting cause and effect*
- Cause-and-effect chart
- Text types: *Biography, social studies article*
- Literary element: *Characterization*

Writing:
- Giving advice
- Informal e-mail messages
- Self-evaluation
- Editorial checklist

Listening/Speaking:
- Giving advice
- Group discussion

Grammar:
- Modals

Viewing/Representing:
- Maps, illustrations

ACADEMIC CONTENT
- Social studies vocabulary
- Sor Juana Inés de la Cruz
- The Peace Corps

BACKGROUND

Sor Juana Inés de la Cruz is a biography of a famous Mexican poet and writer.

Make connections Juana Inés Ramírez de Asbaje lived in Mexico in the 1600s. She was a very intelligent child. She could read and write by age six or seven, but she never went to school. Later, she became a nun and changed her name to Sor Juana Inés de la Cruz. She wrote some of the greatest poems in the Spanish language. Her life story is a great example of the power of the human spirit.

1. How do you think Juana Inés was able to learn so much without going to school?
2. How was life for Juana Inés different from life for girls and young women today in this country?

66

LEARN KEY WORDS

advice
approve of
criticizing
defended
dowry
encouragement
epidemic
remarkable

VOCABULARY

Read these sentences. Use the context to figure out the meaning of the **red** words. Use a dictionary to check your answers. Write each word and its meaning in your notebook.

1. She didn't know what to do about her problem, so she asked her aunt for **advice**.
2. Unfortunately, her parents didn't **approve of** the man she wanted to marry.
3. Most of the people liked his speech, but a few people wrote letters **criticizing** his ideas.
4. Sor Juana strongly **defended** her opinions when they were attacked.
5. Juana Inés's family didn't have money for a **dowry**, so it was unlikely that she would marry.
6. Because of her teacher's **encouragement**, Jean is now studying to be a doctor.
7. If the country experiences a flu **epidemic**, many people might die.
8. Sor Juana was a **remarkable** person. She did things that were difficult for women of her time to do.

READING STRATEGY

Making Inferences

Making inferences, or **inferring,** is making logical guesses based on what the author tells you. Your own knowledge and experience will help you make these guesses.

Biography

As you read this biography, notice some of the inferences you make. What does the author tell you directly about Sor Juana and her surroundings? What details do you fill in based on your knowledge and experience?

SOR JUANA INÉS DE LA CRUZ

Kathleen Thompson

In the foothills of the volcano Popocatépetl in Mexico, there is a village called San Miguel Nepantla. In that village in 1648, or perhaps 1651, a little girl was born. She was poor and she never knew her father, but one day she would be the greatest poet in Mexico.

Juana Inés Ramírez de Asbaje grew up in her grandfather's house with her mother and two sisters. Her grandfather was a gentle man who loved books and learning. From the beginning of her life, little Juana Inés felt the same way. When she was only three years old, she **begged and pleaded** to

---

begged and pleaded, asked for something again and again

get one of her older sister's teachers to give her lessons. From somewhere, she heard that eating cheese made people slow to learn. This isn't true, of course. But even though Juana Inés loved cheese, she **gave it up.** By the time Juana Inés was six or seven, she could read and write well, but she wanted to learn more. She asked her mother to let her dress up as a boy so that she could go to the university, where girls were not allowed.

As you can imagine, her mother said "No." So Juana Inés spent her time in her grandfather's library, reading all his books. Once she set herself to the task of learning grammar. When she didn't learn it fast enough, she cut off a lot of her hair. When she was still too slow—in her own opinion—she cut her hair even shorter. She felt that a head should not be "**adorned** with hair and **naked** of learning."

When Juana Inés was about nine years old, her grandfather died. Not long after, Juana Inés went to live with her aunt and uncle in Mexico City. It was very different from San Miguel. Her uncle, Juan de Mata, was very rich. He and his wife, Doña María, were friends of the viceroy, the governor of Mexico, or New Spain, as it was then called. There were many **luxuries** in the Mata house.

However, the most important difference for Juana Inés was that in Mexico City, she had a chance to learn more than she ever could just from her grandfather's library.

---

gave it up, stopped eating it
adorned, decorated
naked, empty or bare
luxuries, expensive things that people want but don't really need

Juana Inés stayed with her aunt and uncle until she was fifteen. Then, they took her to the viceroy's **court.** A new viceroy and his wife, the vicereine, had just arrived from Spain. When the vicereine, Leonor Carreto, met Juana Inés, she immediately liked the bright, pretty teenager. She asked Juana Inés to live in the **palace** and be one of her personal **attendants.**

Juana Inés and Leonor, who was exactly twice Juana Inés's age, became good friends. They talked together constantly about art and ideas and music. When Juana Inés started writing poetry, Leonor gave her advice and encouragement.

Life at the viceregal court was very lively. There were dances and plays and concerts. There was also a lot of romance. Although Juana Inés was beautiful and intelligent, there was no chance that she would marry one of the young men who gathered around her. She was too poor.

---

court, the buildings and grounds where the viceroy and vicereine live and work
palace, large house where the viceroy and vicereine live
attendants, people who work for and take care of the viceroy and vicereine

---

BEFORE YOU GO ON . . .

1. What did Juana Inés ask her mother to do so she could go to the university?
2. How was her life in Mexico City different from life where Juana Inés was born?

HOW ABOUT YOU?
- When you were younger, what was something you really wanted to learn? How did you learn it?

In those days, no young man in court society would ever marry a young woman unless she had a dowry. When a marriage took place, the bride was expected to bring a large sum of money with her to the marriage. Without a dowry, there would be no marriage. Juana Inés had no dowry.

One day, Juana Inés would have to decide what she was going to do in a world where there were no careers for women and where marriage to an educated man who could share her interests was not possible for her.

Soon, Juana Inés's remarkable mind became so famous that the viceroy set up a little test for her. He called to the palace forty of the most **learned** men in the city. They were scientists and mathematicians, poets and philosophers—men from every branch of learning. They were invited to question seventeen-year-old Juana Inés.

The questions **flew thick and fast**. Juana Inés answered, argued, and answered some more. No one could **stump** her. The forty scholars left, **stunned** by the knowledge and intelligence of the remarkable young woman.

A little more than a year later, Juana Inés became a nun. She entered the **convent** of San Jerónimo. Her name was now Sor Juana Inés de la Cruz: Sister Juana Inés of the Cross.

In those days, being a nun was not the same as it is today. For one thing, to

---

learned, educated or having a lot of knowledge
flew thick and fast, came quickly and close together
stump, confuse (slang)
stunned, amazed
convent, place where nuns live

become a nun, a woman had to pay the convent a dowry, just as if she were getting married. The dowry for Juana Inés was paid by a rich man who supported many young men and women who became priests and nuns. Also, the convent was made up of "cells" that were sold or rented to the nuns. The cell that was bought for Juana Inés had a bedroom, living room, kitchen, and bathroom. Over the years, she collected a huge number of books, works of art, and musical and scientific instruments.

Sor Juana's day began at six o'clock in the morning with prayers and then Mass, the Catholic church service. At eight, she had breakfast in her cell. At nine, there were more prayers. Later in the morning, all the nuns spent some time sewing, either alone or in small groups. At noon, there were prayers before lunch. At three, there were prayers followed by a rest period, or siesta. At sunset, the nuns had a snack of fresh or preserved fruit. At seven, there were prayers and then dinner. Then there was **recreation** until prayers before bed.

Most of Sor Juana's time was spent studying or writing.

The nuns in the convent of San Jerónimo were not allowed to go outside its walls. However, many people from the palace of the viceroy and from other rich households came to visit the nuns. The nuns entertained them with music or with good conversation.

Because of her learning and her personality, Sor Juana had many visitors, including scientists and writers. She talked to them with great cleverness about life and literature. She made up poems **on the spot** in different languages. She played word games and participated in the court **gossip**.

Sor Juana often wrote poems to celebrate special occasions at court. In return, she was given expensive presents, and the convent was given special **favors**. Therefore, the convent encouraged her to write for the court.

Sor Juana wrote two long plays—one of them a comedy. She also wrote many short comedies, dramas, and religious plays. Everything she wrote was excellent.

---

recreation, something done for fun

---

on the spot, done without planning or preparation
gossip, talk about other people
favors, support or advantages or rights given to someone by someone else

BEFORE YOU GO ON . . .

1. How did the viceroy test Juana Inés? How well did she do on his test?
2. In which genres did Sor Juana write?

HOW ABOUT YOU?

• What do you find most interesting about Sor Juana? Why?

Although she spent most of her life in the convent, Sor Juana wrote with beauty and understanding about the joy and suffering of love. She created a poetic world and a poetic language all her own. She became one of the greatest poets ever to write in Spanish.

For many years, Sor Juana's life continued the same way. However, there were men in the church who did not approve of the **brilliant** nun. They did not think she should be allowed to write about anything but religion. However, Sor Juana's friends in the viceroy's court always protected her.

Then, two leaders of the church started a **feud**, and Sor Juana was **caught in the middle**. The bishop of Puebla asked Sor Juana to write a letter criticizing a

sermon that had been written forty years before by a priest named Father Antonio Vieyra. The bishop knew that the criticism would make the archbishop angry because he was a great admirer of Father Vieyra.

Sor Juana wrote the letter, and the bishop had it published. The bishop wrote an introduction to the letter. However, he signed it with the name of a nun, Sor Filotea, so that the archbishop would not know that he had written it. In the introduction, he said that Sor Juana should spend more of her time writing about "holy matters" because she did it so well.

Sor Juana's criticism of Vieyra's sermon did indeed make the archbishop angry. He became even angrier when Sor Juana wrote a long answer to "Sor Filotea" explaining why she wrote what she did.

Sor Juana defended her interest in learning by saying that all knowledge leads to God. She also defended the rights of women to study, write, and participate in the world of ideas.

---

brilliant, very intelligent
feud, a fight or conflict that lasts a long time
caught in the middle, stuck between two sides

This made the archbishop furious. As it happened, the archbishop had a terrible fear of women. He said that if a woman even entered his house, he would have the bricks she stepped on removed. He thanked God that he was **nearsighted** so that he wouldn't have to see women.

Even so, Sor Juana might have won her fight, but **fate** stepped in.

About this time, there was a famine. The people began to riot because there was not enough food. During this famine, the archbishop proved to be more effective than the viceroy. The people obeyed him instead of the viceroy, and they made it through the famine. The archbishop's power increased.

One of the first ways the archbishop used his new power was to **put pressure on** Sor Juana to stop her writing. The viceroy and his court could no longer defend her.

After a long struggle, Sor Juana had to give in. One of the most brilliant thinkers in the Americas allowed her great library of books to be sold. One of the greatest influences on the culture of her time **retired from** society and spoke no longer with her fellow writers and artists. The greatest poet Mexico had ever known **put away her pen**.

Shortly afterward, an epidemic struck the convent, and Sor Juana died while caring for her fellow nuns.

---

retired from, left; gave up
put away her pen, stopped writing

About the Author

Kathleen Thompson

Kathleen Thompson is the author of more than 100 books for young adults, including *Portrait of America*, which has been serialized for television. She has received numerous awards for her work, including Best Books for Youth from the American Library Association in 1974 and the Gold Camera Award from the U.S. Industrial Film Festival.

LITERARY ELEMENT

Characterization is the process a writer uses to create and develop the characters in a story. Characterization can be either direct or indirect.

When using the direct method, the writer states the character's traits. When using the indirect method, the reader must make inferences based on what the character says and does, or based on what others say about him or her.

---

nearsighted, unable to see things clearly unless they are very near
fate, a power that some believe controls what happens to them in their lives
put pressure on, try to force

BEFORE YOU GO ON . . .

1. What rights of women did Sor Juana defend?
2. Why did Sor Juana finally stop writing?

HOW ABOUT YOU?
- What is something you love to do? How would you feel if you had to give it up?

Review and Practice

One way to remember facts is to think about cause and effect as you are reading a text. Here is an example of cause and effect:

cause	effect
I ran six miles,	so I was tired.

Reread the biography of Sor Juana. Then copy the cause-and-effect chart into your notebook and complete it.

Cause	Effect
Sor Juana heard that eating cheese made it harder to learn.	Sor Juana stopped eating cheese.
The vicereine, Leonor Carreto, liked Juana Inés.	
Juana Inés had no dowry.	
Two church leaders had a long-standing dispute.	
Sor Juana defended the rights of women.	
The archbishop put pressure on Sor Juana to stop writing.	

1. Choose one of the people you read about in the text. Write a paragraph about the person. In your paragraph, tell whether you like or dislike the person, and why.

2. Many things have changed since Sor Juana's time. How has life changed since the time your parents or grandparents were young? Think about these topics: education, career opportunities, dowries, and epidemics. Ask an older relative or family friend about these topics.

Discuss in pairs or small groups.

1. Make a list of adjectives that describe Sor Juana. Do you think these traits describe a person whose life is a good example of the human spirit?

2. Do you think Sor Juana was happy at the viceroy's house? Why or why not? What does the text say that supports your inference?

3. How do you think Sor Juana felt about giving up her books and writing?

4. If Sor Juana lived today, what kind of work do you think she would do? Why?

This is an article about the Peace Corps, an organization that helps people all over the world. Read this article and think about how the Peace Corps is another example of the human spirit at work.

The Peace Corps

Shortly after John F. Kennedy became president in 1961, he established the Peace Corps. The Peace Corps is an **agency** that **promotes** world peace and friendship. Volunteers from the United States work in communities in **developing** countries. They help these communities improve social, educational, and economic conditions. Peace Corps volunteers help to build schools; they teach; they help farmers; they help to bring clean water to communities; they work to stop the spread of AIDS and other diseases. These are just a few examples of the ways volunteers try to help.

---

agency, an organization, especially with a government, that does a specific job
promotes, helps something develop and be successful
developing, growing or changing into a country with a lot of industry

A Peace Corps volunteer teaching ▼

More than 165,000 Americans have joined the Peace Corps, and they have worked in more than 100 countries. Volunteers must be at least eighteen years old. But adults of all ages join, including **senior citizens**. Volunteers receive language and cross-cultural training when they go to the countries where they will work. They are expected to speak the local language, to respect the customs of the people they work with, and to **adapt** to the living conditions of the communities in which they work.

One of the goals of the Peace Corps is to help give the people in developing countries the education and training needed to take care of their own futures. The Peace Corps tries to **focus** on the most important needs of the countries where the organization is active. For example, in countries where most people need to get their food directly from their land, the focus is on farming and agriculture, rather than business or education.

▲ Some Peace Corps volunteers help communities with agricultural work.

Since 1995, the Peace Corps has also worked with the International Rescue Committee (IRC). Together, the IRC and the Peace Corps help **refugees** by providing useful training such as farming methods that don't **harm** the environment. The countries where the two organizations have worked together include Tanzania, Rwanda, and Burundi in Africa.

---

senior citizens, people over sixty-five years old
adapt, change your behavior because of a new situation you are in
focus, concentrate; place importance
refugees, people who have to leave their own countries, especially because of a war
harm, hurt

BEFORE YOU GO ON . . .

1 What are some things Peace Corps volunteers do?

2 How do volunteers prepare for their work?

HOW ABOUT YOU?

• Do you do volunteer work? If so, what kind of work is it?

Some people criticize the Peace Corps because they think volunteers don't receive enough training. They think Peace Corps volunteers do not stay long enough in the countries they visit to really understand local problems. Some people also believe that Americans should spend their time and energy working on problems here in our own country.

Some volunteers actually do try to help make life better for others here in the United States. They believe their experience in other countries helps them to do this. Volunteers learn many things from the people in their host countries. Often, when they return to the United States, they continue to promote peace and understanding. There is a program called The Peace Corps Fellows/USA that helps volunteers get **scholarships** for master's degree programs when they return. In exchange, the returned volunteers teach or work in other areas such as public health. The Peace Corps also helps Americans understand different cultures and countries. For example, some returned volunteers visit schools and talk to students about their experiences. Students have the opportunity to ask volunteers questions about places they are studying.

Now, more than ever, we realize how **interconnected** we all are, here on our planet. Peace Corps volunteers and the people they work and live with help to strengthen these connections.

The IRC helps people who are leaving a country because they are being harmed because of their race, culture, or religion. They also help people whose countries have been struck by war or violence. They provide medical services and a safe place for people to live.

▲ Peace Corps volunteers at the playground they helped build

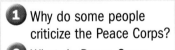

BEFORE YOU GO ON . . .

1 Why do some people criticize the Peace Corps?

2 What do Peace Corps volunteers sometimes do when they get home?

HOW ABOUT YOU?
- What kind of Peace Corps work do you think helps the most?

---

scholarships, money given to students to help pay for their education
interconnected, linked together

78

Link the Readings

REFLECTION

Reread "The Peace Corps," and think about *Sor Juana Inés de la Cruz.* Copy the chart into your notebook and complete it.

Title of Selection	Genre	Fiction or Nonfiction	Purpose of Selection	Demonstration of the Human Spirit
Sor Juana Inés de la Cruz				
"The Peace Corps"				

DISCUSSION

Discuss in pairs or small groups.

1. Would you like to spend two years in the Peace Corps? Why or why not?

2. Peace Corps volunteers serve people by teaching skills that are necessary for life. Do you think people like Sor Juana—poets and scholars—also serve their communities? Compare these two kinds of work.

3. In Sor Juana's day, many people had opinions about the roles and rights of women that would not be popular today. In some places where Peace Corps workers volunteer, local people have different opinions about the rights and roles of women. What should Peace Corps workers do about this? Should they "accept" the host country's beliefs, or should they take a stand based on their own beliefs?

Connect to Writing

GRAMMAR

Using Modals of Advice

When giving advice, use the **modals** *should, shouldn't, had better,* and *had better not*. Modals go before the base form of a verb.

Use *should* to give advice about what is the right thing to do.

> Peace Corps volunteers **should** get more training.

Use *shouldn't* to give advice about what is the wrong thing to do.

> Peace Corps volunteers **shouldn't** ignore the customs of the people they work with.

Had better and *had better not* are stronger than *should*. These modals imply that something bad might happen if you don't follow the advice.

> The people **had better** get food (or they will riot).
> Sor Juana **had better not** enter the archbishop's house (or he will remove the bricks she stepped on).

Use *I think* or *Maybe* before a sentence with a modal of advice to be more polite.

> **I think**
> **Maybe** you should study French before you go to France.

Practice

Copy the paragraph into your notebook. Add the modals *should, shouldn't, had better,* or *had better not*.

> Do you like to travel to foreign countries? If so, these tips will be helpful. First, you _____ carry cash. Somebody might steal it. Instead, you _____ take traveler's checks. You _____ keep a copy of the serial numbers separate from the traveler's checks. Second, you _____ keep your passport in a safe place. Third, you _____ learn enough "survival" words and phrases in the country's language in case you get lost. It's also nice to be able to communicate with people you meet, so you _____ learn some simple social language.

SKILLS FOR WRITING

Giving Advice in an Informal E-Mail Message

Sometimes e-mail is used to give and receive advice. E-mail is often informal. Rules for writing paragraphs don't always apply to e-mail messages.

Address **Attach** **Save** **Print** **Send**

Reply-To: Jennifer Rosario	**Attachments:**
To: Jean Sugihara	

Typeface ▼ **Size ▼** **B** *I* <u>U</u> ☰ ☰ ☰ **Spell Check**

Subject: Your trip!

Hey! I hear you are going to Padre Island for the summer! I was there last year. Had a great trip. But I had one BIG problem–I got really sunburned!!!!

May I give you some advice?

You should get a strong sun block lotion, and wear it whenever you go out. You should also wear a hat and sunglasses or the sun could damage your eyes. You'd better take lots of shorts and tank tops, because you'll die of the heat if you wear jeans or long-sleeved shirts. And you should drink lots of water, even if you're not thirsty, because your body loses a lot of water in the heat. You shouldn't spend time outside between 11:00 a.m. and 2:00 p.m. unless you have to.

Gotta go! Have fun! And take a lot of pictures!

Jennifer

---

1. What does the writer tell her friend she should do?
2. What does the writer tell her friend she shouldn't do?
3. What reasons does the writer give for her advice?
4. Does the writer use formal or informal language? Give examples.

WRITING ASSIGNMENT

Advice in an Informal E-Mail Message

You will give advice to a friend in an informal e-mail message. Give a friend suggestions about traveling to your region.

1. **Read** Reread the e-mail message on page 81. What advice does the writer give her friend?

Writing Strategy: Advice Chart

You can use a chart to help you organize your ideas. First, write the topic or problem above the chart. Then make the chart. Write **Should** at the top of the left column. Write **Shouldn't** at the top of the right column. Then list your suggestions in the chart.

Look at the advice chart for the e-mail message on page 81.

How to Avoid Sunburn

Should	Shouldn't
get sunblock lotion wear a hat and sunglasses	spend time outside between 11:00 a.m. and 2:00 p.m.

---

2. **Make an advice chart** Make an advice chart in your notebook. What should people do if they visit your region? Write it in the left side of the chart. What shouldn't they do? Write it in the right side of the chart.

3. **Write an e-mail message** Use your advice chart to write an informal e-mail message to a friend.

EDITING CHECKLIST

Did you . . .

▶ give the reader advice about what to do and what not to do?

▶ give reasons for your advice?

▶ use friendly, informal language?

Check Your Knowledge

Language Development

1. Describe how you make inferences while you read.

2. How can a cause-and-effect chart help you understand a text? How can it help you prepare to write?

3. What is a biography? What biographies have you read?

4. What is characterization? What is the difference between direct characterization and indirect characterization?

5. What kind of words do you use when you give someone advice? Give an example of a sentence in which you give advice.

Academic Content

1. What new social studies vocabulary did you learn in Part 2? What do the words mean?

2. Who was Sor Juana Inés de la Cruz? What kind of education did she have?

3. What is the Peace Corps? Why did President Kennedy create it? What kind of work do Peace Corps volunteers do?

The Peace Corps

Put It All Together

OBJECTIVES

Integrate Skills
- Listening/ Speaking: *Group presentation*
- Writing: *Letter to the editor*

Investigate Themes
- Projects
- Further reading

LISTENING and SPEAKING WORKSHOP

GROUP PRESENTATION

You will give a group presentation telling about a person you admire.

1 **Think about it** Make a list of people you admire. Think about these questions: How does this person reflect the human spirit? What has he or she done to help other people, overcome hardships, or otherwise demonstrate the human spirit? Make a list of each person's qualities.

Work in small groups. Compare your lists of people and qualities. Choose one person from your lists.

2 **Organize** As a group, decide what information about your person each group member will present. Write notes about your part of the presentation. Don't write everything you will say, word for word. Write the main ideas only. Then look at your notes briefly as you speak to remind you of what you want to say.

3 **Practice** Decide the order in which group members will speak. Practice each part of the presentation, using your notes. Make suggestions for improvement, if necessary.

4 **Present and evaluate** Give your presentation to the class. As each group finishes, evaluate the presentation. Did you understand the speakers? What did you like best about the presentation? Do you have suggestions for improvement?

SPEAKING TIP

When using notes in a presentation, be sure to look up and speak to your audience. Refer to your notes when you need to, but keep your eyes on your listeners as much as possible.

LISTENING TIPS

- Give each speaker your attention. Make eye contact with the speaker, and don't talk to your classmates.
- Respect each speaker. Listen politely, even if you disagree with the speaker's ideas.

WRITING WORKSHOP

LETTER TO THE EDITOR

People write letters to the editors of newspapers to express their opinions about something. Sometimes a writer describes a problem in the community and suggests how the problem might be solved. The writer tries to convince the reader of his or her position.

A good letter to the editor includes the following characteristics:

- an opening paragraph with a clear statement of the writer's opinion
- facts and/or examples that support the writer's opinion presented in a clear, organized way
- a concluding paragraph that restates the writer's main idea in a different way and offers a solution

You will write a letter to the editor of your school or local newspaper. Use the following steps and the model on page 86 to help you.

1 **Prewrite** Brainstorm some issues that you feel strongly about. Possible issues might include the school dress code, boys' and girls' sports, cafeteria food, pollution in your city or town—anything you care about. Make a list of issues.

Then read your list. Choose one issue that you feel most strongly about. Use a main-idea-and-details chart to organize your ideas about the issue.

Before you write a first draft of your letter, read the following model. Notice the characteristics of a letter to the editor.

January 23, 2004 ←— **Date**

To the Editor: ←———————————— **Greeting**

    I am writing about the problem of pollution in our community. It's disgraceful that people dump glass, plastic, and other garbage in our parks, forests, and rivers. In addition, factory exhaust pollutes the air.

> **The writer states the issue and her opinion about it.**

    Our community is home not only to people, but also to many other living things that have thrived here for millennia. These plants and animals have as much right to live here as we do. It is our duty to respect the environment as our home and theirs. Pollution is not only ugly, but it also kills and causes health problems for all the living things in our environment.

> **She gives details to support her argument.**

    We all have a responsibility to protect and preserve the environment. We need to remind people not to litter. Our police need to enforce laws against pollution. Parents need to teach their children to dispose of garbage properly. And we should all recycle our used glass, plastic, and paper. I believe that taking these actions will help us keep our community freer from pollution.

> **She offers a solution and restates her opinion in a different way.**

Sincerely, ←—— **Closing**

Natalia Dare ←—— **Name**

2 **Draft** Use your main-idea-and-detail chart and the model to write your letter to the editor.

- In your opening paragraph, state the issue and your opinion about it.

- Give facts or examples to support your opinion. Try to persuade the reader of your position.

- In your concluding paragraph, offer a solution and restate your opinion in a different way.

WRITING TIP

When you write a letter expressing your opinion, be polite. Try to focus on ways to solve the problem rather than dwelling on the problem itself.

3 **Edit** Work in pairs. Trade papers and read each other's letters. Use the editing checklist to evaluate your work.

EDITING CHECKLIST

Did you . . .

- ▶ state your opinion clearly and politely?
- ▶ use supporting facts and examples?
- ▶ use correct letter format?
- ▶ use adjectives and adverbs correctly?
- ▶ use dependent and independent clauses correctly?
- ▶ use correct spelling, capitalization, and punctuation?

4 **Revise** Revise your letter. Add information and correct mistakes, if necessary.

5 **Publish** Share your letter with your teacher and classmates.

PROJECTS

Work in pairs or small groups. Choose one of these projects.

1 Create a large "human spirit timeline" in your classroom. Draw pictures of people or groups whose lives and work have reflected the human spirit throughout history. Write a short paragraph that tells why each person or group belongs on the timeline.

2 Interview someone in your community or in your school who has worked hard to help others or to overcome obstacles. Prepare for your interview by writing your questions. If possible, invite the person to your school so the class can ask questions. If this isn't possible, use a tape recorder to be sure you don't miss anything. Share your interview with the class.

3 Write a poem or a song about Abraham Lincoln, Sor Juana Inés de la Cruz, or another famous person you admire. Read your poem or sing your song for your class.

4 Use the Internet or library to research a person whose life is an example of the human spirit. Write a short biography telling the important events in the person's life based on what you learn.

5 Present a "human spirit award" to someone in your school. Work with other students who want to recommend someone for the award. Write a persuasive argument telling why the person you chose deserves the award. Read all the arguments to the class and take a vote. Invite the winner to the class and present that person with the award.

Further Reading

To find out more about the theme of this unit, choose from these reading suggestions.

The Lotus Seed, **Sherry Garland** A Vietnamese girl fleeing her war-torn country takes a lotus seed to remind her of her homeland. Many years later, her grandson plants the dried-up seed, and a beautiful lotus blossom appears. It is a symbol of the grandmother's past and her determination to keep the traditions of her homeland alive.

Only Passing Through: The Story of Sojourner Truth, **Anne Rockwell** This is the true story of a former slave who used her own experiences to speak out about the evils of slavery. In doing so, Sojourner Truth became an important voice in the fight to end slavery.

Black Star, Bright Dawn, **Scott O'Dell** When her father is injured, Bright Dawn takes his place in the Iditarod, a 1,000-mile dogsled race through Alaska's frozen wilderness. Faced with dangers of all kinds, she must learn to keep going in spite of her fears.

Nelson Mandela, **Coleen Degnan-Veness** This biography focuses on Mandela's fight to achieve equality for black people in South Africa. Early in his career, Mandela was accused of trying to overthrow the white government and was put in jail. But he could not be silenced. In 1994, after twenty-seven years in prison, Nelson Mandela became South Africa's first black president.

Maya Lin, Architect, **Bettina Ling** In 1981, Maya Lin won a national contest to design a monument dedicated to the veterans of the Vietnam War. This biography describes her struggles to get the monument built. It also discusses her other works, including her memorial to the Civil Rights movement in the United States.

VOICES OF FREEDOM

We The People

EQUAL RIGHTS FOR ALL AMERICANS

PART 1
- "I Have a Dream," Martin Luther King Jr.
- "Lady Freedom Among Us," Rita Dove

PART 2
- From *Roll of Thunder, Hear My Cry*, Mildred D. Taylor
- "Words of Freedom"

The wish to live in freedom was one important reason for the American Revolution. Freedom continues to be an essential value for U.S citizens. Freedom is closely linked to equal treatment for all. If people do not have equal opportunities in education, employment, and other areas of life, they are not living in freedom.

In Part 1, you will read a famous speech by Martin Luther King Jr., a leader who accomplished great things for people in this country. You will also read a poem about freedom.

In Part 2, you will read a story about two African-American children who were treated unfairly because of their race. Finally, you will read about some of the documents that guarantee freedom to people who live in the United States.

91

Prepare to Read

BACKGROUND

"I Have a Dream" is a famous speech by Dr. Martin Luther King Jr. A speech is a talk given in front of an audience about a particular subject. The speaker usually talks about his or her ideas and opinions. Often, the purpose of a speech is to persuade the audience of something.

Make connections Martin Luther King Jr. was a minister who was an important leader in the 1950s and 1960s—a time when African Americans were struggling to achieve equality in the United States. In both northern and southern states, African Americans faced greater difficulties than white people in education, jobs, and housing.

In the 1950s, many people in the United States worked together for equality. Their struggle is known as the Civil Rights movement. Dr. Martin Luther King Jr. was one of the movement's most important leaders. He taught Americans to fight injustice without the use of violence. Tragically, in 1968, Dr. King was shot and killed in Memphis, Tennessee.

1. What was the Civil Rights movement? When did it start?
2. What was an important part of how Dr. King taught people to fight injustice?
3. How and when did Dr. King die?

Thousands gathered in the nation's capital on August 28, 1963, to hear civil rights leaders speak. ▶

LEARN KEY WORDS

character
discrimination
justice
oppression
poverty
revolt
segregation

VOCABULARY

Read these sentences. Use the context to figure out the meaning of the **red** words. Use a dictionary to check your answers. Write each word and its meaning in your notebook.

1. Dr. King's courage, faith, and determination showed his strong **character**.
2. Racial **discrimination** by employers is illegal. Employees of all races must be treated equally.
3. **Justice**, or fairness, is the goal of our legal system.
4. Although slaves were freed after the Civil War, they still had to fight **oppression**. They were denied equal rights in housing, employment, and education.
5. Many African Americans were unable to get jobs and earn money. The result was that they faced **poverty**.
6. If a government treats people unfairly, the people may **revolt** against that government.
7. The schools in the South practiced **segregation**. There were separate schools for African-American and white children.

READING STRATEGY

Summarizing

Summarizing a text is restating the main ideas in your own words. Summarizing can be especially helpful if the text is difficult or the ideas are new or complicated.

- As you read, stop frequently and restate what the writer is saying.
- When you finish reading the text, try to restate the author's main points.
- Try to remember details that support the main points.
- Always keep in mind your purpose for reading the text.

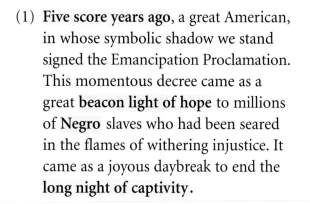

Preview Dr. King's speech. What kind of "dream" does Dr. King have? Now read the speech carefully. Stop after each paragraph to summarize the main idea.

I Have a Dream

Martin Luther King Jr.

(1) **Five score years ago,** a great American, in whose symbolic shadow we stand signed the Emancipation Proclamation. This momentous decree came as a great **beacon light of hope** to millions of **Negro** slaves who had been seared in the flames of withering injustice. It came as a joyous daybreak to end the **long night of captivity.**

(2) But one hundred years later, we must face the tragic fact that the Negro is still not free. One hundred years later, the life of the Negro is still sadly **crippled by the manacles of segregation** and the chains of discrimination. One hundred years later, the Negro lives on a lonely island of poverty in the midst of a vast ocean of material prosperity.

(3) One hundred years later, the Negro is still **languishing** in the corners of American society and finds himself an **exile** in his own land. So we have come today to dramatize an appalling condition.

five score years ago, one hundred years ago
beacon light of hope, something that guides and encourages people
Negro, African American (a word used in the past, now considered offensive)
long night of captivity, long period of slavery
crippled by the manacles of segregation, prevented from living freely because of racial discrimination

LITERARY ELEMENT

A *metaphor* compares two things without using the word *like* or *as.* Dr. King uses many metaphors in his speech. For example, in paragraph 2: . . . *the Negro is still sadly crippled by the . . . chains of discrimination.* In this metaphor, discrimination is compared with chains. Dr. King is saying that discriminating against African-American people is keeping them in chains.

languishing, suffering
exile, a person forced to leave his or her own country

(4) In a sense we have come to our nation's capital to cash a check. When the architects of our republic wrote the magnificent words of the Constitution and the Declaration of Independence, they were signing a promissory note to which **every American was to fall heir**. This note was a promise that all men would be guaranteed the **inalienable** rights of life, liberty, and the pursuit of happiness.

(5) It is obvious today that America has defaulted on this promissory note insofar as her **citizens of color** are concerned. Instead of honoring this sacred obligation, America has given the Negro people a bad check, which has come back marked "insufficient funds." But we refuse to believe that the bank of justice is bankrupt. We refuse to believe that there are insufficient funds in the great vaults of opportunity of this nation. So we have come to cash this check—a check that will give us upon demand the riches of freedom and the security of justice. We have also come to this hallowed spot to remind America of the fierce urgency of now. This is no time to engage in the luxury of cooling off or to take the **tranquilizing drug of gradualism**. Now

▲ Dr. King giving his speech "I Have a Dream"

---

every American was to fall heir, every U.S. citizen would receive

inalienable, cannot be given or taken away

citizens of color, nonwhite U.S. citizens

tranquilizing drug of gradualism, the idea that equality should be achieved slowly over a long period of time

BEFORE YOU GO ON . . .

1 In paragraph 1, what came as a "great beacon light of hope"?

2 Reread paragraph 4. What promise did the Constitution and the Declaration of Independence make to all U.S. citizens?

HOW ABOUT YOU?

● What are your feelings as you read the speech?

is the time to rise from the dark and desolate valley of segregation to the sunlit path of racial justice. Now is the time to open the doors of opportunity to all of God's children. Now is the time to lift our nation from the quicksand of racial injustice to the solid rock of brotherhood.

(6) It would be fatal for the nation to overlook the urgency of the moment and to underestimate the determination of the Negro. This sweltering summer of the Negro's legitimate discontent will not pass until there is an invigorating autumn of freedom and equality. Nineteen sixty-three is not an end, but a beginning. Those who hope that the Negro needed to **blow off steam** and will now be content will have a rude awakening if the nation returns to business as usual. There will be neither rest nor tranquility in America until the Negro is granted his citizenship rights. The whirlwinds of revolt will continue to shake the foundations of our nation until the bright day of justice emerges.

(7) But there is something that I must say to my people who stand on the warm threshold, which leads into the palace of justice. In the process of gaining our rightful place we must not be guilty of wrongful deeds. Let us not seek to satisfy our thirst for freedom by drinking from the cup of **bitterness** and hatred.

(8) We must forever conduct our struggle on the high plane of dignity and discipline. We must not allow our creative protest to **degenerate** into physical violence. Again and again we must rise to the majestic heights of meeting physical force with soul force. The marvelous new militancy which has engulfed the Negro community must not lead us to distrust all white

---

blow off steam, let out anger

bitterness, anger
degenerate, collapse; disintegrate

people, for many of our white brothers, as evidenced by their presence here today, have come to realize that their destiny is tied up with our destiny and their freedom is inextricably bound to our freedom. We cannot walk alone.

(9) And as we walk, we must make the pledge that we shall march ahead. We cannot turn back. There are those who are asking the devotees of civil rights, "When will you be satisfied?" We can never be satisfied as long as our bodies, heavy with the fatigue of travel, cannot gain lodging in the motels of the highways and the hotels of the cities. We cannot be satisfied as long as the Negro's basic **mobility** is from a smaller ghetto to a larger one. We can never be satisfied as long as a Negro in Mississippi cannot vote and a Negro in New York believes he has nothing for which to vote. No, no, we are not satisfied and we will not be satisfied until justice rolls down like waters and righteousness like a mighty stream.

---

mobility, ability to move easily from one place to another

(10) I am not unmindful that some of you have come here out of great **trials and tribulations**. Some of you have come fresh from narrow **cells**. Some of you have come from areas where your quest for freedom left you battered by storms of **persecution** and staggered by the winds of police **brutality**. You have been the veterans of creative suffering. Continue to work with the faith that **unearned suffering is redemptive**.

(11) Go back to Mississippi, go back to Alabama, go back to Georgia, go back to Louisiana, go back to the slums and ghettos of our modern cities, knowing that somehow this situation can and will be changed. Let us not wallow in the valley of despair.

---

trials and tribulations, difficulties
cells, small rooms where prisoners are kept
persecution, cruel or unfair treatment; discrimination
brutality, cruelty; viciousness
unearned suffering is redemptive, you will be rescued from undeserved or unjust pain

BEFORE YOU GO ON . . .

1 What must African Americans not do in their fight for equality, according to paragraph 7?

2 According to paragraph 9, when will we be satisfied?

HOW ABOUT YOU?
- Do you think this speech is effective? Why or why not?

◀ In 1965, protesters marched 50 miles, from Selma, Alabama, to Montgomery.

▲ Martin Luther King Jr. at the signing of the Civil Rights Act, which made racial discrimination illegal

(12) I say to you today, my friends, that in spite of the difficulties and frustrations of the moment, I still have a dream. It is a dream deeply rooted in the American dream.

(13) I have a dream that one day this nation will rise up and live out the true meaning of its creed: "We hold these truths to be self-evident: that all men are created equal."

(14) I have a dream that one day on the red hills of Georgia the sons of former slaves and the sons of former slaveowners will be able to sit down together at a table of brotherhood.

(15) I have a dream that one day even the state of Mississippi, a desert state, sweltering with the heat of injustice and oppression, will be transformed into an oasis of freedom and justice.

(16) I have a dream that my four children will one day live in a nation where they will not be judged by the color of their skin but by the content of their character.

(17) I have a dream.

(18) I have a dream that one day the state of Alabama, whose governor's lips are presently dripping with the **words of interposition and nullification**, will be transformed into a situation where little black boys and black girls will be able to join hands with little white boys and white girls and walk together as sisters and brothers.

(19) I have a dream today.

(20) I have a dream that one day every valley shall be exalted, yes, every hill and mountain shall be made low, the rough places will be made plain, and the crooked places will be made straight, and the glory of the Lord shall be revealed, and all flesh shall see it together.

(21) This is our hope. This is the faith with which I return to the South. With this faith we will be able to hew out of the mountain of **despair** a stone of hope. With this faith we will be able to transform the jangling **discords** of our nation into a beautiful symphony of brotherhood. With this faith we will be able to work together, to pray together, to struggle together, to go to jail together, to stand up for freedom together, knowing that we will be free one day.

---

words of interposition and nullification, attempts to prevent and reverse progress
despair, sadness; hopelessness
discords, conflicts; fights

▲ Today, all over the United States, people celebrate the birthday of Dr. Martin Luther King Jr.

(22) This will be the day when all of God's children will be able to sing with a new meaning. "My country 'tis of thee, sweet land of liberty, of thee I sing. Land where my fathers died, land of the pilgrim's pride, from every mountainside, let freedom ring."

(23) And if America is to be a great nation this must become true. So let freedom ring from the **prodigious** hilltops of New Hampshire. Let freedom ring from the mighty mountains of New York. Let freedom ring from the heightening Alleghenies of Pennsylvania!

(24) Let freedom ring from the snowcapped Rockies of Colorado!

---

prodigious, huge

(25) Let freedom ring from the **curvaceous** peaks of California!

(26) But not only that; let freedom ring from Stone Mountain of Georgia!

(27) Let freedom ring from Lookout Mountain of Tennessee!

(28) Let freedom ring from every hill and every molehill of Mississippi. From every mountainside, let freedom ring.

(29) When we let freedom ring, when we let it ring from every village and every hamlet, from every state and every city, we will be able to speed up that day when all of God's children, black men and white men, Jews and Gentiles, Protestants and Catholics, will be able to join hands and sing in the words of the old **Negro spiritual**, "Free at last! free at last! thank God almighty, we are free at last!"

---

curvaceous, having curves
Negro spiritual, a type of religious song that was created by slaves in the southern United States

BEFORE YOU GO ON . . .

1 Reread paragraph 16. What is Dr. King's dream for his children?

2 In your own words, describe another of Dr. King's dreams.

HOW ABOUT YOU?
- Do you think any of Dr. King's dreams have come true? If so, which?

Review and Practice

Copy the chart into your notebook. Complete it with a partner. Then use your chart to tell your partner about the speech "I Have a Dream."

Question Word	Answer
Who	Dr. Martin Luther King Jr.
What	"I Have a Dream" speech
Where	
When	
Why	

People in Seattle march on Dr. King's birthday. ▼

EXTENSION

1. Listen to Dr. King's speech. What does his voice tell you about his message? Was Dr. King confident or hopeless about the chance for freedom for all?

2. What is the main idea or point of the speech? What is Dr. King's purpose for giving the speech?

3. Make a list of some words and phrases that Dr. King repeats again and again. Why do you think he repeats them?

DISCUSSION

Discuss in pairs or small groups.

1. It's important to be able to tell the difference between fact and opinion in a speech. Facts can be proven. Opinions are people's feelings about things. Read the following statements and determine whether each is a fact or an opinion.

   - Abraham Lincoln signed the Emancipation Proclamation in 1862.
   - Abraham Lincoln was a great American.

2. Look at the following metaphors from the "I Have a Dream" speech. Then read the paragraph in which the metaphor occurs. If there are words that you don't understand, find their meanings. Then, explain the meaning of the metaphors.

   - "This sweltering summer of the Negro's legitimate discontent will not pass until there is an invigorating autumn of freedom and equality." (paragraph 6)
   - "Some of you have come from areas where your quest for freedom left you battered by storms of persecution. . . ." (paragraph 10)
   - "With this faith we will be able to transform the jangling discords of our nation into a beautiful symphony of brotherhood." (paragraph 21)

Poetry

Like Dr. King's speech, Rita Dove's poem "Lady Freedom Among Us" reminds us of the importance of freedom. Like Dr. King, the poet has used metaphors to make her point in an interesting way. As you read the poem, notice that the language does not always follow capitalization and punctuation rules.

◀ This statue, *Freedom*, is the subject of Rita Dove's poem, "Lady Freedom Among Us." The statue usually sits at the top of the Capitol building in Washington, D.C. When it was taken down to be cleaned, Dove saw it on the ground and was inspired to write the poem.

Lady Freedom Among Us

▲ The statue *Freedom*

don't lower your eyes
or stare straight ahead to where
you think you ought to be going

don't **mutter** *oh no*
not another one
get a job fly a kite
go bury a bone

with her old-fashioned sandals
with her **leaden** skirts
with her stained cheeks and whiskers
    and heaped up trinkets
she has risen among us in **blunt reproach**

she has fitted her hair under a hand-me-down cap
and spruced it up with feathers and stars
slung over one shoulder she bears
the rainbowed layers of charity and **murmurs**
all of you even the least of you

don't cross to the other side of the **square**
don't think *another item to fit on a tourist's agenda*
consider her drenched gaze her shining brow
she who has brought mercy back into the streets
and will not retire politely to the **potter's field**

---

mutter, speak or say words unclearly; mumble
leaden, made of lead; heavy
blunt reproach, clear blame or disapproval
murmurs, whispers
square, an open place in a town with buildings all around it
potter's field, a burial place for very poor, unknown people

BEFORE YOU GO ON . . .

1. The poem's title includes the name of the statue—*Freedom*. Do you think the poem is about the statue? Explain.

2. Look at the statue *Freedom*. What words in the poem seem to describe the statue?

HOW ABOUT YOU?
- Would you like to see the statue *Freedom*? Why or why not?

103

having assumed the thick skin of this town
its gritted exhaust its sunscorched and **blear**
she rests in her weathered **plumage**
bigboned **resolute**

don't think you can ever forget her
don't even try
she's not going to **budge**

no choice but to grant her space
crown her with sky
for she is one of the many
and she is each of us

                              Rita Dove

---

blear, dim; sore
plumage, the feathers of a bird
resolute, determined; firm
budge, move; go away

About the Author

Rita Dove

Rita Dove was born in 1952 in Ohio. She studied literature in the United States and in Germany. She received the Pulitzer Prize in poetry in 1987. In 1993, at the age of forty, she was the youngest person and the first African American to become the Poet Laureate of the United States. One of Dove's goals as a poet is for poetry to become a household word.

A family of immigrants at Ellis Island ▼

BEFORE YOU GO ON . . .

1 What two things are being compared in the metaphor "crown her with sky"?

2 The last line of the poem says that "she is each of us." What is Lady Freedom compared with in this metaphor?

HOW ABOUT YOU?

- This poem is asking us not to forget about how important freedom is. In what ways is freedom important to you?

Link the Readings

Look at "I Have a Dream" again and reread "Lady Freedom Among Us." Copy the chart into your notebook and complete it.

Title of Selection	Genre	Purpose of Selection	One Idea from the Text
"I Have a Dream"			
"Lady Freedom Among Us"		*to entertain and instruct*	

DISCUSSION

Discuss in pairs or small groups.

1. The statue *Freedom* stands for the idea of freedom. The Statue of Liberty and the Liberty Bell also represent freedom. What other symbols of freedom can you think of?

2. Martin Luther King Jr. and Rita Dove both use the word *freedom*. Do they use this word in the same way? What does Martin Luther King Jr. mean by *freedom*? What does Rita Dove mean by *freedom*?

3. What elements of poetry are there in the "I Have a Dream" speech?

▲ The Liberty Bell in Philadelphia, Pennsylvania

Connect to Writing

GRAMMAR

The Present Perfect

Remember to use the **simple past** to talk about actions that happened at a specific time in the past:

> Rita Dove **wrote** "Lady Freedom Among Us" in 1993.

Use the **present perfect** to talk about actions that happened at an indefinite time in the past:

> Rita Dove **has written** many poems.

Use the present perfect to talk about actions that started in the past and continue into the present (with *for* or *since*):

> I **have enjoyed** Rita Dove's poetry for many years.
>
> I **have enjoyed** Rita Dove's poetry since 1997.

Use the present perfect with *ever* to ask if the person has done something "at any time" or "in your entire life":

> **Have** you ever **read** Rita Dove's poems?

Form the present perfect with *have* or *has* and the **past participle**. For regular verbs, the past participle is formed by adding *-ed* to the base form of a verb.

> Past participles of regular verbs: **worked   played   laughed   stayed**

Irregular verbs do not have *-ed* in the past participle.

> Past participles of irregular verbs: **read   written   heard   been**

Practice

Copy these sentences into your notebook. Choose the correct verb.

1. The themes in Dove's poetry are themes she (wrote / has written) about for years.
2. We (heard / have heard) Dr. King's speech yesterday.
3. They (worked / have worked) to end discrimination when they were students.
4. You (read / have read) many interesting texts since you began this book.
5. Dr. King (was / has been) a very great leader.

SKILLS FOR WRITING

Writing Essays

An essay is a short nonfiction work about a topic.

Yevong Dekhang

Technology has changed a lot in the last fifty years. My friend Peggy was a child during the 1950s. She remembers when there were no computers for personal use. There were computers at some companies, but they were huge, not like the PCs we use today. Most families owned no more than one car, and few families owned TVs.

Of all the advances in technology, PCs have changed Peggy's life the most. With the Internet, she keeps in touch with friends and family members, and makes reservations in hotels around the world. She even plays games on her PC.

When I asked Peggy if life was better then or now, she said she likes the present better. If we were still living in the 1950s, traveling around the world would not be so easy. She does wish that families could spend more time together rather than work all the time. But, on the whole, she believes that her life has changed for the better.

1. What is the main idea of the essay?
2. Which paragraph includes details that support the main idea?
3. Find a sentence that uses the present perfect. Why did the writer use the present perfect in this sentence?

WRITING ASSIGNMENT

Descriptive Essay

You will write an essay describing an important way in which life has changed over the years for someone much older than yourself.

1. **Read** Look at the model on page 107. Think of someone you would like to interview about how life has changed for him or her. Ask the person to describe what has changed most over the years. Record his or her responses.

Writing Strategy: Outline

An outline can help you organize your ideas for your essay. Look at the outline the writer made before writing the essay on page 107. She states her main ideas (*A, B*), and then lists descriptive details that support the main ideas (*1, 2, 3*).

> A. Technology has changed a lot in the last 50 years.
>   1. Peggy was a child in the 1950s.
>   2. There were no PCs.
>   3. Families owned 1 car, no TV.
>
> B. A PC has changed Peggy's life the most.
>   1. She makes hotel reservations on-line.
>   2. She chats with family and friends.
>   3. She plays games on her PC.

2. **Make an outline** Using the model, make an outline for your descriptive essay. Use letters to list the main ideas and numbers to list the supporting details.

3. **Write** Use your outline to write your essay. Start each paragraph with a main idea. Then use the descriptive details to support the main idea.

EDITING CHECKLIST

Did you . . .

▶ include one or more main ideas?

▶ include details to support the main ideas?

▶ use the present perfect correctly?

Check Your Knowledge

Language Development

1. What do you do to summarize? How can this help you as you read?
2. What is the purpose of a speech? Of a poem?
3. What is a metaphor? Give an example.
4. How do you form the present perfect? Use a present-perfect verb in a sentence.
5. How can an outline help you organize main ideas and details when you write?
6. What is one thing that a speech and an essay have in common?
7. How does the photograph of the statue *Freedom* help your understanding of the poem?

Academic Content

1. What new social studies vocabulary did you learn in Part 1? What do the words mean?
2. What do you know about Dr. Martin Luther King Jr.?
3. What is the Civil Rights movement? When did it start?

Prepare to Read

OBJECTIVES

LANGUAGE DEVELOPMENT

Reading:
- Vocabulary building: *Context, dictionary skills*
- Reading strategy: *Visualizing*
- Text types: *Historical fiction, social studies article*
- Literary element: *Mood*

Writing:
- Brainstorming
- Poetry

Listening/Speaking:
- Understand main points from discussion
- Compare and contrast

Grammar:
- Gerunds and infinitives

Viewing/Representing:
- Photographs

ACADEMIC CONTENT

- Social studies vocabulary
- Constitution, Declaration of Independence, Bill of Rights
- Structure of U.S. government

BACKGROUND

The passage you will read is from a novel entitled *Roll of Thunder, Hear My Cry.* The novel is historical fiction. The story deals with racism—treating some people differently from others because of their race.

Make connections Before 1954, it was legal for schools and other public places to be segregated, or separated, by race as long as the places were "equal." To determine if schools were "equal," people would look at the school building, furniture, books, and materials. In 1954, the U.S. Supreme Court, the highest court in the United States, ruled that "separate" cannot be "equal." Just the fact that the races were kept segregated made the schools or other places unequal.

This passage from *Roll of Thunder, Hear My Cry* takes place in the 1930s, in Mississippi, long before the 1954 Supreme Court ruling. The setting—a segregated school attended by African-American children—is historical. The characters Cassie and her brother, Little Man, are fictional.

Discuss the questions.
1. What can happen when students don't get an adequate education?
2. Do you think the condition of your school building, equipment, and materials is important to your education? Why or why not?

LEARN KEY WORDS

disappointment
fiercely
fortunate
indignant
startling
tense
tolerate

VOCABULARY

Read these sentences. Use the context to figure out the meaning of the **red** words. Use a dictionary to check your answers. Write each word and its meaning in your notebook.

1. When she saw how dirty the book was, her excitement turned to **disappointment**.
2. The teacher warned her students not to go near the dog because it was growling **fiercely**.
3. The students never had books before, and they felt **fortunate** to get them.
4. He felt that he was treated unfairly, and he was very upset and **indignant**.
5. The loud noise in the quiet classroom was **startling** to everyone.
6. The teacher and the principal were both angry, and this made the students upset and **tense**.
7. Her behavior was so bad that the teacher could not **tolerate** it, and he sent her home.

READING STRATEGY

Visualizing

Visualizing means picturing something in your mind. Writers have many ways to help readers visualize what they read. Often they use adjectives and adverbs. But other words, such as nouns and verbs, also can help readers visualize.

As you read, let your mind form pictures of the characters, action, and setting in the text. Visualizing the story can help you understand it better and enjoy it more.

Historical Fiction

Before you begin reading, preview the text. Then, as you read, use the visualizing strategy to help you picture what is happening. Try to imagine Miss Crocker, the students, and the scene in the classroom. What words help you visualize?

from Roll of Thunder, Hear My Cry

Mildred D. Taylor

Now Miss Crocker made a startling announcement: This year we would all have books.

Everyone gasped, for most of the students had never handled a book at all besides the family Bible. I admit that even I was somewhat excited. Although Mama had several books, I had never had one of my own.

"Now we're very fortunate to get these readers," Miss Crocker explained while we eagerly awaited the **unveiling.** "The county superintendent of schools himself brought these books down here for our use and we must take extra-good care of them." She moved toward her desk. "So let's promise that we'll take the best care possible of these new books." She stared down, expecting our response. "All right, all together, let's repeat, 'We promise to take good care of our new books.'" She looked sharply at me as she spoke.

"WE PROMISE TO TAKE GOOD CARE OF OUR NEW BOOKS!"

"Fine," Miss Crocker **beamed**, then proudly threw back the **tarpaulin.**

Sitting so close to the desk, I could see that the covers of the books, a motley red, were badly worn and that the gray edges of the pages had been **marred** by pencils, crayons, and ink. My **anticipation** at having my own book **ebbed** to a sinking disappointment. But Miss Crocker continued to beam as she called each fourth grader to her desk and, recording a number in her roll book, handed him or her a book.

As I returned from my trip to her desk, I noticed the first graders anxiously watching the disappearing pile. Miss Crocker must have noticed them too, for as I sat down she said, "Don't worry, little ones, there are plenty of readers for you too. See there on Miss Davis's desk." Wide eyes turned to the covered teacher's platform directly in front of them and an **audible** sigh of relief swelled in the room.

I glanced across at Little Man, his face lit in **eager** excitement. I knew that he could not see the soiled covers or the marred pages from where he sat, and even though his **penchant** for cleanliness was often annoying, I did not like to think of his disappointment when he saw the books as they really were. But there was nothing I could do about it, so I opened my book to its center and began browsing through the spotted pages. Girls with blond braids

---

audible, loud enough to be heard
eager, enthusiastic
penchant, liking or fondness

---

unveiling, presentation
beamed, had a big smile
tarpaulin, a piece of material used to cover or protect things
marred, ruined
anticipation, excitement
ebbed, grew less; weakened

BEFORE YOU GO ON . . .

1 What announcement does Miss Crocker make to the class?

2 What does the narrator notice about the books on the desk?

HOW ABOUT YOU?

- Did you visualize as you read this page? What pictures did you see in your mind?

and boys with blue eyes stared up at me. I found a story about a boy and his dog lost in a cave and began reading while Miss Crocker's voice droned on **monotonously**.

Suddenly I grew conscious of a break in that monotonous tone and I looked up. Miss Crocker was sitting at Miss Davis's desk with the first-grade books stacked before her, staring fiercely down at Little Man, who was pushing a book back upon the desk.

"What's that you said, Clayton Chester Logan?" she asked.

The room became gravely silent. Everyone knew that Little Man was in big trouble for no one, but no one, ever called Little Man "Clayton Chester" unless she or he meant serious business.

---

monotonously, boringly; tediously

114

LITERARY ELEMENT

Texts express feelings of happiness, sadness, tension, seriousness, or other emotions. This is the text's *mood*. The writer creates the mood by using words that evoke these feelings. What mood does this sentence create: *The room became gravely silent*?

Little Man knew this too. His lips parted slightly as he took his hands from the book. He **quivered**, but he did not take his eyes from Miss Crocker. "I—I said may I have another book please, ma'am," he squeaked. "That one's dirty."

"Dirty!" Miss Crocker echoed, **appalled** by such **temerity**. She stood up, gazing down upon Little Man like a bony giant, but Little Man raised his head and continued to look into her eyes. "Dirty! And just who do you think you are, Clayton Chester? Here the county is giving us these wonderful books during these hard times and you're going to stand there and tell me that the book's too dirty? Now you take that book or get nothing at all!"

Little Man lowered his eyes and said nothing as he stared at the book. For several moments he stood there, his face barely visible above the desk, then he turned and looked at the few remaining books and, seeming to realize that they were as badly soiled as the one Miss Crocker had given him, he looked across the room at me. I nodded and Little Man, glancing up again at Miss Crocker, slid the book from the edge of the desk, and with his back straight and his head up returned to his seat.

---

quivered, shook with emotion
appalled, horrified, surprised, and angry
temerity, boldness; lack of respect

Miss Crocker sat down again. "Some people around here seem to be **giving themselves airs**. I'll tolerate no more of that," she scowled. "Sharon Lake, come get your book."

I watched Little Man as he scooted into his seat beside two other little boys. He sat for a while with a **stony** face looking out the window; then, evidently accepting the fact that the book in front of him was the best that he could expect, he turned and opened it. But as he stared at the book's inside cover, his face clouded, changing from sulky acceptance to puzzlement. His brows furrowed. Then his eyes grew wide, and suddenly he sucked in his breath and sprang from his chair like a wounded animal, flinging the book onto the floor and stomping madly upon it.

---

giving themselves airs, acting more
    important than they are
stony, without expression or feeling; like a
    stone

BEFORE YOU GO ON . . .

1. How do the students know that Little Man is in trouble?
2. Why does Little Man want a different book?

HOW ABOUT YOU?

- Do you think Little Man was wrong to ask for a different book? Why or why not?

Miss Crocker rushed to Little Man and grabbed him up in powerful hands. She shook him **vigorously,** then set him on the floor again. "Now, just what's gotten into you, Clayton Chester?"

But Little Man said nothing. He just stood staring down at the open book, shivering with indignant anger.

"Pick it up," she ordered.

"NO!" defied Little Man.

"No? I'll give you ten seconds to pick up that book, boy, or I'm going to get my **switch.**"

Little Man bit his lower lip, and I knew that he was not going to pick up the book. Rapidly, I turned to the inside cover of my own book and saw immediately what had

made Little Man so **furious.** Stamped on the inside cover was a chart which read:

PROPERTY OF THE BOARD OF EDUCATION Spokane County, Mississippi September, 1922		
Date of Issuance	Condition of Book	Race of Student
1. September 1922	New	White
2. September 1923	Excellent	White
3. September 1924	Excellent	White
4. September 1925	Very Good	White
5. September 1926	Good	White
6. September 1927	Good	White
7. September 1928	Average	White
8. September 1929	Average	White
9. September 1930	Average	White
10. September 1931	Poor	White
11. September 1932	Poor	White
12. September 1933	Very Poor	nigra
13.		
14.		
15.		
16.		
17.		
18.		
19.		
20.		

The blank lines continued down to line 20 and I knew that they had all been reserved for black students. A knot of anger swelled in my throat and held there. But as Miss Crocker directed Little Man to bend over the "whipping" chair, I put aside my anger and jumped up.

"Miz Crocker, don't please!" I cried. Miss Crocker's dark eyes warned me not to say another word. "I know why he done it!"

---

vigorously, strongly
switch, a thin stick used at that time to hit a child as punishment

---

furious, very angry; enraged

"You want part of this switch, Cassie?"

"No'm," I said **hastily**. "I just wanna tell you how come Little Man done what he done."

"Sit down!" she ordered as I hurried toward her with the open book in my hand.

Holding the book up to her, I said, "See Miz Crocker, see what it says. They give us these ole books when they didn't want 'em no more."

She regarded me **impatiently,** but did not look at the book. "Now how could he know what it says? He can't read."

"Yes'm, he can. He been reading since he was four. He can't read all them big words, but he can read them columns. See what's in the last row. Please look, Miz Crocker."

This time Miss Crocker did look, but her face did not change. Then, holding up her head, she gazed unblinkingly down at me.

"S-see what they called us," I said, afraid she had not seen.

"That's what you are," she said coldly. "Now go sit down."

I shook my head, realizing now that Miss Crocker did not even know what I was talking about. She had looked at the page and had understood nothing.

"I said sit down, Cassie!"

I started slowly toward my desk, but as the hickory stick sliced the tense air, I turned back around. "Miz Crocker," I said, "I don't want my book neither."

The switch landed hard upon Little Man's upturned bottom. Miss Crocker looked questioningly at me as I reached up to her desk and placed the book upon it. Then she swung the switch five more times and, discovering that Little Man **had no intention of** crying, ordered him up.

"All right, Cassie," she sighed, turning to me, "come on and get yours."

---

had no intention of, would refuse to

About the Author

Mildred D. Taylor

Mildred D. Taylor was born in Jackson, Mississippi, in 1943. Taylor has taken many of the ideas for her stories from her own life. Two of the subjects she often writes about are family unity and racism.

BEFORE YOU GO ON . . .

1 What makes Little Man so angry?

2 Why does Miss Crocker punish Cassie?

HOW ABOUT YOU?

- Describe the mood in this scene. How does the scene make you feel?

---

hastily, hurriedly; quickly
impatiently, with annoyance or irritation

Review and Practice

Reread the excerpt from *Roll of Thunder, Hear My Cry* and think about the events that make up the story's plot. Then read the list of events. The events are not in the order in which they happened in the story. Copy the chart into your notebook and rewrite the events in the correct order.

Events: Cassie shows Miss Crocker the inside cover of her book.

Miss Crocker tells Cassie to come and get her punishment.

Little Man flings his book onto the floor and stomps on it.

~~Miss Crocker announces that the children are getting books.~~

Miss Crocker punishes Little Man with her switch.

Little Man asks for another book because his is dirty.

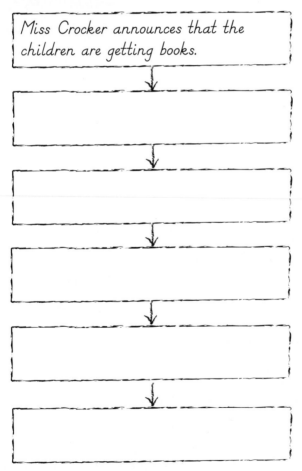

Miss Crocker announces that the children are getting books.

Compare charts in pairs or small groups. Revise your chart if necessary. Then take turns using your charts to retell the story.

118

EXTENSION

With a partner, talk about what Cassie and Little Man went through during their day at school. How is their life at school different from yours? How is their life just like yours? Write a paragraph comparing your day at school with theirs. When you have finished writing, trade papers with another pair of students and read each other's work.

DISCUSSION

Discuss in pairs or small groups.

1. How do you think Cassie feels about the fact that her book has pictures of children with blond hair and blue eyes?
2. If you were Little Man, would you take the book? Why or why not?
3. What makes Cassie decide to refuse her book?

▲ Children in school, 1930s

Social Studies

This is an informational text about three very important documents in American history—the Declaration of Independence, the Constitution, and the Bill of Rights. They date back to the time of the American Revolution, and they were instrumental in establishing this country.

Words of Freedom

The Declaration of Independence (July 4, 1776)

By 1776, the American colonists realized that they needed to become independent from Great Britain. On July 4, the colonists **broke all their ties** with Britain. They formally announced their independence from Britain in the Declaration of Independence. The thirteen colonies immediately became thirteen American states. The main author of the Declaration of Independence was Thomas Jefferson, a lawyer and farmer from Virginia who later became the third president of the United States.

Two of the most important ideas expressed in the Declaration of Independence are that all people are "created equal" and that all people are entitled to "life, liberty, and the **pursuit** of happiness."

The belief in the equality of all people is central to the idea of **democracy** in the United States. The Declaration of Independence has inspired many people to fight for equality and to be tolerant of others.

▲ Thomas Jefferson, author of the Declaration of Independence and the third U.S. president

---

broke all their ties, ended their relationship with
pursuit, ability to have
democracy, a form of government in which citizens can vote to elect
    officials

The Constitution (1788)

After the United States won its independence from Britain, Americans faced a new challenge. The thirteen new states needed to find a way to work together as one country. Using **principles** from the Declaration of Independence, the Founding Fathers wrote the Constitution. This document forms the basis of the U.S. government.

The Constitution describes the organization of the national government. It divides the government into three parts, or branches:

- The legislative branch: This is the Congress. It makes the laws for the country.

- The executive branch: The president is the head, or chief, of this branch. It **enforces** laws made by Congress and controls the nation's military and foreign policy.

- The judicial branch: The Supreme Court is the head of this branch. The judicial branch **interprets** the laws that Congress passes and makes sure that the laws follow the principles of the Constitution.

The Constitution of the United States ▼

BEFORE YOU GO ON . . .

1. What happened on July 4, 1776?
2. What are two important ideas in the Declaration of Independence?

HOW ABOUT YOU?
- What are two interesting facts that you learned about the Constitution and the Declaration of Independence?

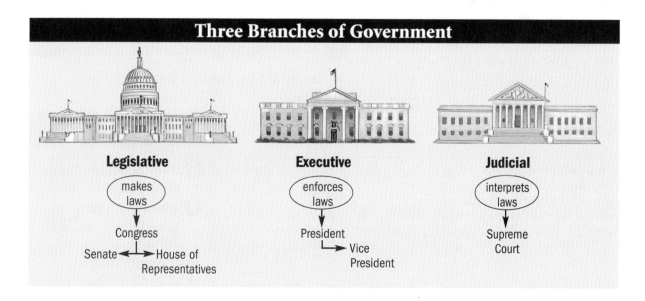

Three Branches of Government

Legislative	Executive	Judicial
makes laws	enforces laws	interprets laws
Congress	President	Supreme Court
Senate ◄─► House of Representatives	└► Vice President	

principles, main beliefs or values
enforces, carries out; makes happen
interprets, explains what something, such as a document, means

The Founding Fathers wanted to be certain that no one branch of government had more power than another. They established what is called the system of checks and balances. Each branch of government has some—but not total—power over the other two branches. In 1788, the Constitution of the United States became law, and in 1789, George Washington was elected the first president of the United States.

The Bill of Rights (1791)

Many citizens were concerned that the Constitution created a strong national government, but did not protect the basic rights of people. As a result, ten amendments, or additions, were added to the Constitution. These amendments are called the Bill of Rights.

The Bill of Rights **guarantees** personal rights such as freedom of religion, freedom of speech, freedom of the press, and a fair trial in court. The rights in the Bill of Rights form the **foundation** of American democracy. This was the first time that a country wrote a constitution that promised to protect the individual **civil** and **political rights** of all its free citizens.

▲ The Bill of Rights protects the rights of every U.S. citizen.

guarantees, promises
foundation, basis; the most important part
civil, of the government, state, or nation
political, relating to the government or politics of a country
rights, freedoms and advantages that people have

BEFORE YOU GO ON . . .

1 What concerned citizens about the Constitution?

2 What are two rights guaranteed by the Bill of Rights?

HOW ABOUT YOU?

● What do you think is the most important protection in the Bill of Rights? Why?

Link the Readings

Look at the excerpt from *Roll of Thunder, Hear My Cry* and reread "Words of Freedom." Copy the chart into your notebook and complete it.

Title of Selection	Genre	Fiction or Nonfiction	Purpose of Selection	Important Issue(s)
From Roll of Thunder, Hear My Cry				*equality*
"Words of Freedom"			*to inform*	

DISCUSSION

Discuss in pairs or small groups.

1. If your class received worn and dirty books, how would you feel? What would you do to change the situation?

2. In what ways did Cassie and Little Man show that they had courage and pride? Did you admire what they did? Why or why not?

3. What do the main characters' experiences show about the ideas of equality at that time, in that place?

Connect to Writing

GRAMMAR

Gerunds and Infinitives

Gerunds and **infinitives** are verbs that act like nouns. Gerunds are formed by using the base form of the verb + **-ing**. Some verbs, such as *swim* and *run,* double the final consonant before adding **-ing**.

Infinitives are formed by using **to** + the base form of the verb.

Gerunds	Infinitives
They love **singing**.	They like **to sing**.
I like **swimming**.	I like **to swim**.

Some verbs can be followed by either a gerund or an infinitive. Some of these verbs are *begin, love, like, hate, prefer.*

> She **loves to read** in bed.
> She **loves reading** in bed.

Some verbs can only be followed by a gerund. Some of these verbs are *enjoy, quit, finish, suggest, keep.*

> I **enjoy fishing.**
> My mother **kept reading.**

Some verbs can only be followed by an infinitive. Some of these verbs are *hope, plan, need, want, ask.*

> I **hope to be** a veterinarian when I grow up.
> He **wants to go** to the movies.

Practice

Write the sentences in your notebook using the correct form of the verb. If both forms are correct, write the sentence with each form.

1. My friends love (to discuss / discussing) politics.
2. She wants (to become / becoming) a teacher someday.
3. He prefers (to read / reading) books about history.
4. I enjoy (to write / writing) poetry about my country.
5. He suggested (studying / to study) together.

SKILLS FOR WRITING

Writing a Poem

When you write a poem, you have more freedom with language than when you write a paragraph or an essay. Poets use words in an interesting way to create images, sounds, and rhythms.

Read this poem. Then discuss the questions that follow it.

Kate Younkins

Song of Freedom

The robin sings a bell-like tune
Whose ringing echoes in the ear —
A song that goes with sounds of June,
All a-buzz with life most dear.

Canary has to sing her song
Inside a cage — poor locked up bird!
Her voice is clear, but something's wrong,
It fades away before it's heard.

---

1. What is the poem about?
2. Read the poem aloud. What sounds are important to the poem?
3. How does the poet feel about the subject?
4. How is the format of the poem different from the form of a paragraph?
5. Are there any gerunds or infinitives?

WRITING ASSIGNMENT

Poem

You will write a poem about an important value or principle that helps people live together peacefully. Examples include equality, loyalty, and freedom.

1. **Read** Reread the student model on page 125. You might also wish to look again at the poem "Lady Freedom Among Us," pages 103–104, for ideas. Choose an important principle to write your poem about.

Writing Strategy: Brainstorming

One way to brainstorm is to list all the ideas in your mind that relate to your topic. Don't worry if the ideas don't make sense. Just keep writing. You can even draw pictures. Here are the student's notes for her poem about freedom:

2. **Brainstorm** Write your topic in your notebook and quickly list ideas about it. Sketch drawings if you can't think of exact words.

3. **Write** Use your brainstorming notes to write your poem. Include some gerunds and infinitives.

EDITING CHECKLIST

Did you . . .

▶ use language in an interesting way to create images?

▶ use gerunds and infinitives correctly?

▶ read your poem aloud to make sure you like the way it sounds?

Check Your Knowledge

Language Development

1. Describe two images you visualized as you read the excerpt from *Roll of Thunder, Hear My Cry.*

2. What makes *Roll of Thunder, Hear My Cry* historical fiction?

3. What is the mood of *Roll of Thunder, Hear My Cry*? Give an example of something the author does to create this mood.

4. Imagine that a friend is writing a poem. Explain to your friend how brainstorming can help him or her think of ideas for the poem.

5. Give examples of sentences containing infinitives and gerunds.

Academic Content

1. What new social studies vocabulary did you learn in Part 2? What do the words mean?

2. What is the Declaration of Independence?

3. What kind of government is described in the Constitution?

4. Name two rights guaranteed by the Bill of Rights.

◀ The Declaration
of Independence

Put It All Together

LISTENING and SPEAKING WORKSHOP

OBJECTIVES

Integrate Skills
- Listening/
  Speaking:
  Speech
- Writing:
  *Descriptive
  essay*

**Investigate
Themes**
- Projects
- Further
  reading

SPEECH

You will give a speech describing what freedom means to you.

1 **Think about it** Ask yourself: What does freedom mean to me? Am I free? Does everyone in the world today have freedom? Write short answers to these questions. Work in small groups. Compare your answers and discuss your ideas.

2 **Organize** Decide which ideas you want to include in your speech about freedom. Write a sentence that tells the main idea of your speech. Then write details that support your main idea. To conclude your speech, write two or three sentences to summarize the ideas you have expressed.

3 **Practice** Practice giving your speech in your group. Other group members can comment on the speech and give suggestions for improvement, if necessary.

4 **Present and evaluate** Each person presents his or her speech to the class. Evaluate the presentations. What did you like best about the speech? Were the speaker's ideas clear and persuasive? Do you have suggestions for improvement?

SPEAKING TIPS

- Use note cards to help you remember the important points of your speech. Don't write your whole speech on the cards. Write key words to help you remember the main ideas.
- Share a personal experience that illustrates your ideas about freedom. Using a personal experience can make your speech more interesting and persuasive.

LISTENING TIPS

- When listening to your classmates' speeches, listen for examples they use to illustrate their ideas about freedom. Think about how these ideas are similar to or different from your own.
- If something a speaker says is not clear, make a note. Wait until the speaker has finished to ask your question.

WRITING WORKSHOP

DESCRIPTIVE ESSAY

In a descriptive essay, the writer uses descriptive details to help the reader picture what someone or something is like. In a description of a person, colorful details help you "see" the person and understand his or her special qualities.

A good descriptive essay includes the following characteristics:

- a main idea stated clearly in the first paragraph
- details and examples in other paragraphs that support the main idea
- colorful verbs, adverbs, and adjectives
- a restatement of the main idea in the last paragraph

You will write a descriptive essay about a person who represents for you some aspect of the idea of freedom. The person can be someone famous, a relative, family member, or friend. Use the model essay and the following steps to help you.

1 Prewrite Write the word *freedom* in the middle of a sheet of paper. Draw a circle around it. What people come to mind when you think of freedom? Write their names around the circle, and make a word web. Think about their special qualities. What obstacles did they overcome? What achievements or contributions have they made? Why do they make you think about freedom?

Choose one person to write about. Make a chart with three columns. In the first column, list the person's special qualities. In the second column, list obstacles he or she overcame. In the third column, list his or her achievements or contributions.

WRITING TIP

When you write a description, choose words that express exactly what you want to say. A thesaurus is a book of words and their synonyms. Computers also usually have an electronic thesaurus for finding synonyms. Use a thesaurus to help you choose specific words to make your descriptions more colorful and interesting.

For example, the lists below of words from a thesaurus show different ways of describing similar things.

Verbs: eat, gobble, munch, devour
Adjectives: excellent, wonderful, outstanding, remarkable, fantastic
Adverbs: quickly, speedily, swiftly, immediately, promptly

Before you write a first draft, read the following model. Notice the characteristics of a descriptive essay.

Natalia Dare

Abraham Lincoln represents freedom to me. Lincoln believed that slavery was wrong and that people should be treated equally. Many Americans violently disagreed with his opinion. When Lincoln was elected president in 1860, the country was divided into free states and slave states. By 1861, eleven slave states had seceded from the United States and formed the Confederacy.

As president, Lincoln led the country in a war to preserve the Union. In 1863, during the war, he wrote the Emancipation Proclamation, declaring that all slaves in the seceded states "are, and henceforward shall be free." Later that year, Lincoln gave his famous Gettysburg Address, in which he proclaimed that the United States would have "a new birth of freedom—and that government of the people, by the people, for the people shall not perish. . . ."

Lincoln's inspiring words gave people hope that the United States would be whole again. Although he did not live to see the end of the war, Lincoln is remembered for his courageous efforts to make the United States truly the "land of the free."

The writer clearly states her main idea in the first paragraph.

She supports her main idea by giving specific examples of what Lincoln did to protect people's freedom.

The writer restates her main idea in a new and interesting way.

2 **Draft** Use the model and your chart to write your personal description.

- In the first paragraph, explain why this person makes you think of freedom. Include a description of the person's special qualities.

- Next, describe an obstacle or problem he or she overcame.

- Then describe his or her important achievements or contributions.

- Conclude your description by restating why the person represents freedom to you.

3 **Edit** Work in pairs. Trade papers and read each other's essays. Use the editing checklist to evaluate your work.

EDITING CHECKLIST

Did you . . .

▸ clearly state your main idea in the first paragraph?

▸ give details and examples to support your main idea?

▸ use colorful details to describe the person and his or her achievements?

▸ use simple-past and present-perfect verbs correctly?

▸ use gerunds and infinitives correctly?

▸ capitalize the first letter of every sentence?

▸ use correct punctuation?

4 **Revise** Revise your essays. Add details and correct mistakes if necessary.

5 **Publish** Share your essay with your teacher and classmates.

Work in pairs or small groups. Choose one of these projects.

1 Use the Internet and other resources to find out more about people who are fighting for equality or freedom in America or in other parts of the world. You could also find out about people who did this in the past. Make a list, draw a picture, write a news story, or give a short oral report to tell what you learned.

2 Talk to a family member or neighbor who was alive when Martin Luther King Jr. gave his speech. Make a list of questions to ask that person. Be sure to include questions about his or her involvement, if any, in the Civil Rights movement. You may also wish to ask how the movement changed America, and how the Civil Rights movement affected him or her. Share what you learn with the class.

3 Read *Roll of Thunder, Hear My Cry* or another of Mildred D. Taylor's books. As you read, write your thoughts and feelings in a journal. Tell what you like or don't like about the plot or the characters. Also include any questions you have about what you are reading.

4 Make a collage about freedom. Find pictures in magazines and newspapers that represent freedom to you and paste them onto a sheet of construction paper. You can include your own pictures. Hang your collage up in your classroom.

5 The Constitution and the Bill of Rights tell about the rights and protections people have in the United States. Find out about the rights of people who live in other countries. What documents describe people's rights? How are their rights the same as or different from the rights of people who live in the United States?

Further Reading

To find out more about the theme of this unit, choose from these reading suggestions.

Frederick Douglass: Portrait of a Freedom Fighter, **Sheila Keenan** Frederick Douglass was a former slave who became a noted abolitionist, speaker, and author. This biography helps us understand the times in which he lived.

The Big Lie: A True Story, **Isabella Leitner** This book uses simple language to tell the story of the author's horrifying experiences during the Nazi takeover of Poland and Hungary. As a girl, Isabella and her family are thrown into cattle cars and taken to Nazi camps. Against all odds, Isabella survives the concentration camps, miraculously escapes, and lives to tell this haunting tale.

F is for Freedom, **Roni Schotter** Amanda has no idea that her home is a stop on the Underground Railroad. Suddenly her parents have guests—a family of fugitive slaves, including Hannah, a girl of about Amanda's age. In the time they spend together, Amanda and Hannah form a lasting friendship and learn a lot about the value of freedom.

Journey to Ellis Island: How My Father Came to America, **Carole Bierman** This is the true story of a boy who escaped from Russia to find freedom in America. The book includes details about Ellis Island, where many immigrants landed in the early 1900s. It also includes postcards and photographs, which make it seem like a family album.

Number the Stars, **Lois Lowry** In 1943, the Jewish people in Denmark are being forced to "relocate," which means they are being sent to Nazi death camps. Annemarie Johansen's best friend Ellen is Jewish. While Ellen's parents go into hiding, Ellen stays with the Johansens and pretends to be part of the family. This realistic story tells of the strength and courage that people can find when their freedom is at risk.

RISKS and Challenges

PART 1

- "The Train to Freedom"
- "Follow the Drinking Gourd"
- "Five New Words at a Time," Yu-Lan (Mary) Ying

PART 2

- From *The Little Prince: The Play,* Rick Cummins and John Scoullar, adapted from the novel by Antoine de Saint-Exupéry
- "Performance Anxiety"

Taking a risk or accepting a challenge means trying something even though you might fail. There are some risks people should not take. There are also risks worth taking and challenges worth accepting. In this unit, you will meet people who took risks or accepted challenges to improve their lives or to help others.

In Part 1, you will read an article about slaves who risked their lives to escape to freedom and the people who helped them on their way. You will also read about how a mother helped her daughter face a big challenge—learning a new language and adjusting to a new school.

In Part 2, you will read a play about some of the risks involved in making new friends. You will also read about how some people react to the challenge of speaking or performing in front of others.

PART 1

OBJECTIVES

LANGUAGE DEVELOPMENT

Reading:
- Vocabulary building: *Context, dictionary skills*
- Reading strategy: *Skimming for main ideas*
- Text types: *History article, song, personal narrative*

Writing:
- Interview questions
- Self-evaluation
- Editing checklist

Listening/Speaking:
- Appreciation: *Songs*
- Culture: *Oral tradition*
- Listen for major ideas and details
- Interviewing

Grammar:
- Prepositions, prepositional phrases

Viewing/Representing:
- Charts, maps, and photographs

ACADEMIC CONTENT
- Social studies vocabulary
- The Underground Railroad
- Slavery in the United States

Prepare to Read

BACKGROUND

"The Train to Freedom" is a history article. It gives historical information about the Underground Railroad—a network of secret routes that escaping slaves followed to freedom. In the mid-1800s, slavery was illegal in the northern states, but it was still legal in the South. Many slaves in the South tried to escape by following one of the routes of the Underground Railroad. Some people who were against slavery supported the Underground Railroad. They provided food, clothing, and shelter for the escaping slaves.

Make connections Look at the map. It shows some routes slaves took to freedom. Along these routes, there were houses to hide in, places to meet people who would help, and safe places to cross rivers and mountains.

▲ Routes of the Underground Railroad

Look at the map.

1. Follow one of the routes. What states does it go through?
2. What rivers and/or mountain ranges are on the route?
3. What is the longest route? Where does it end?

LEARN KEY WORDS

fugitive
heritage
network
runaway
shelter
spirituals

VOCABULARY

Read these sentences. Use the context to figure out the meaning of the **red** words. Use a dictionary to check your answers. Write each word and its meaning in your notebook.

1. Some **fugitive** slaves were caught and sent back to the places they ran away from.
2. The discoveries, art, events, and accomplishments of our country's past make up our national **heritage**.
3. Free people and slaves were linked together in a **network** of safe hiding places.
4. Some people received rewards for catching and returning **runaway** slaves.
5. People who were against slavery offered their homes as **shelter** to slaves.
6. **Spirituals**, which were originally sung by the slaves, are a treasured part of our culture.

READING STRATEGY

Skimming for Main Ideas

Good readers **skim** a text to help them find the main ideas quickly. Skimming also provides readers with a good opportunity for setting a purpose for reading. Skim the text after you have previewed it. To skim the text:

- Read quickly to get the main ideas. Don't stop at words that you don't understand.

- In each section or paragraph, look for the topic sentence—the sentence that tells you the main idea.

- When you have finished skimming the text, see if you can summarize what it is about.

Then go back and read the text more carefully, paying attention to the details that support the main ideas.

After you preview, skim each section of this text to find the main ideas. Then, read the article more carefully to find details that support the main ideas. Keep in mind your purpose for reading.

The Train to Freedom

Risk Takers

People who tried to escape from slavery in the United States took a dangerous chance. Slave catchers and their dogs **continually** hunted runaway slaves. When they were caught, they might be beaten. Sometimes they were hanged. Even if runaways did not get caught, they often became ill from traveling on foot while tired, cold, wet, and hungry.

---

continually, without stopping

▼ Slaves harvesting cotton

Many free African Americans and others also took risks to help slaves who were running away. People who helped runaways could be punished. Yet many people did not think slavery was right, and they found ways to help the slaves escape.

The Underground Railroad

The Underground Railroad wasn't really underground, and it was not a real railroad. It was called "underground" because it was secret. And it was called a "railroad" because it helped fugitive slaves travel to places where they could be free. A network of people supported the Underground Railroad, helping the slaves escape.

Many of the words connected to the Underground Railroad were railway terms. For example, slaves on the Underground Railroad were called "passengers." The homes, businesses, and churches where they could stop for food or shelter were known as "stations" and "depots." The people who lived in these homes or ran these businesses were called "stationmasters."

"Conductors" were courageous people who went with slaves on their journeys. Levi Coffin, a white **Quaker** from Cincinnati, was a well-known conductor. But the most famous conductor was Harriet Tubman, a woman who had been a slave herself.

▲ Harriet Tubman

Harriet Tubman

Harriet Tubman knew the evils of slavery. She was born a slave and worked as a maid, a children's nurse, and a field worker. When she was in her early teens, she tried to help a runaway slave. When she was caught trying to help, she was hit in the head with a heavy weight and almost died. As a result of this injury, she suffered from **blackouts** throughout her life.

Quaker, a member of a Christian religious group that opposes all forms of violence

blackouts, times when a person loses consciousness

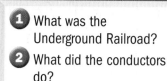

BEFORE YOU GO ON . . .

1 What was the Underground Railroad?

2 What did the conductors do?

HOW ABOUT YOU?

- Do you think it would be more dangerous to be a stationmaster or a conductor? Why?

▲ Harriet Tubman (left) helped many slaves escape to freedom.

Harriet Tubman was twenty-nine years old when she made her own escape from slavery. Her journey was difficult, but she was successful and settled in Philadelphia. She worked as a dishwasher and began to make plans to **rescue** her family. Over the next few years, she brought her sister's family and her brothers to the North, where they were free.

However, Harriet Tubman was still not satisfied. Over a ten-year period, she traveled nineteen times back to the South to help more than 300 slaves escape. She was known along the Underground Railroad as Moses because, like Moses in the story of **Exodus**, she led her people to freedom.

Harriet Tubman became a hero among slaves and among abolitionists, but others hated her. Large rewards were offered for her capture. She wore clever disguises so no one would recognize her.

rescue, save; liberate
Exodus, the second book in the Old Testament of the Bible

Harriet Tubman's accomplishments were not limited to her work on the Underground Railroad. During the Civil War, she became a **spy** for the **Union** army. She later worked in Washington, D.C., as a government nurse. She died at the age of ninety-three.

Travel on the Underground Railroad

What was it like traveling to the North on the Underground Railroad? Although it was different for each person, it was never easy. Slaves had to find out how to escape from the slaveholders' property. Sometimes they had to leave family members or friends and risk never seeing them again. Slaves who wanted to escape could not talk about their plans. Discussing escape plans could be dangerous for the escaping slave or for others.

It was often a challenge for fugitives to find their way from one stop to the next. Sometimes fugitive slaves had a conductor with them from the beginning of the journey, but sometimes they didn't. Runaway slaves had to trust strangers to help them. They often spoke in code, using one word to mean another. (Some of these code words can be found in the spirituals and other slave songs that have become part of our American heritage. The codes used by travelers and helpers on the Underground Railroad could be hidden in these songs.)

Runaway slaves often tried to **cover** between 10 and 20 miles a night. During daylight, they rested at depots or stations—homes, shops, and churches—when they could. Sometimes they slept in barns or in the woods.

The Underground Railroad operated in many states. Ohio, especially, had numerous Underground Railroad stations. Thousands of runaway slaves followed the Underground Railroad into Ohio. To do this they had to cross the Ohio River.

---

spy, someone who watches people secretly to discover facts or information about them
Union, the name used by the northern states during the Civil War
cover, travel

Free States	
California	New Hampshire
Connecticut	New Jersey
Illinois	New York
Indiana	Ohio
Iowa	Oregon
Maine	Pennsylvania
Massachusetts	Rhode Island
Michigan	Vermont
Minnesota	Wisconsin

Slave States	
Alabama	Mississippi
Arkansas	Missouri
Delaware	North Carolina
Florida	South Carolina
Georgia	Tennessee
Kentucky	Texas
Louisiana	Virginia
Maryland	

▲ Free states and slave states in 1860

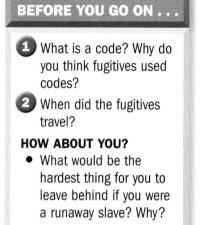

BEFORE YOU GO ON . . .

1. What is a code? Why do you think fugitives used codes?
2. When did the fugitives travel?

HOW ABOUT YOU?

- What would be the hardest thing for you to leave behind if you were a runaway slave? Why?

Other Supporters of the Underground Railroad

Slavery did not occur only in the South of the United States. Many of the slaves brought to North America arrived at northern cities and were sold to slave owners in the North. However, slavery was more **widespread** in the South, and it lasted much longer there.

More and more people in the North heard about the Underground Railroad. They formed groups to raise money and provide food and shelter for runaway slaves. These groups, known as "vigilance committees," helped settle fugitive slaves, who were faced with a very different climate and environment in the North. The vigilance committees helped the former slaves find jobs.

We do not have a complete history of the Underground Railroad. There are few written accounts of the Underground Railroad or the experiences of former slaves. Because of this, no one knows exactly how many slaves escaped on the Underground Railroad to free states, Canada, or Mexico. We also don't know how many people took the risk of helping the fugitive slaves on their way, or who these people were. But some **historians estimate** that as many as 100,000 slaves rode the Underground Railroad to freedom.

---

widespread, in many places; extensive
historians, people who study history
estimate, to guess, based on available information

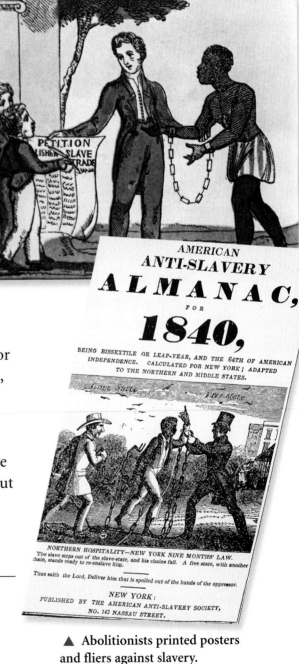

▲ Abolitionists printed posters and fliers against slavery.

Follow the Drinking Gourd

This song contains a secret code. The "drinking gourd" is what the fugitive slaves called the Big Dipper. One of the stars in the Big Dipper points to the North Star, which the fugitive slaves used as a guide to the North.

▲ The Big Dipper

When the sun comes back and the first **quail** calls,
Follow the Drinking Gourd.
For the old man is waiting for to carry you to freedom,
If you follow the Drinking Gourd.

Chorus:
Follow the Drinking Gourd. Follow the Drinking Gourd.
For the old man is awaiting to carry you to freedom if you
Follow the Drinking Gourd.

The river bank makes a very good road,
The dead trees show you the way,
Left foot, **peg foot**, traveling on
Follow the Drinking Gourd.

▲ A dipper is a cup with a long handle. It is used to collect drinking water. The slaves thought of the Big Dipper as a dipper made from a gourd, like this one.

Chorus
The river ends between two hills,
Follow the Drinking Gourd.
There's another river on the other side,
Follow the Drinking Gourd.

Chorus
Where the great big river meets the little river,
Follow the Drinking Gourd.
For the old man is awaiting to carry you to freedom,
If you follow the Drinking Gourd.

---

quail, a wild bird
peg foot, refers to Peg Leg Joe, who went from farm to farm teaching the
  song to slaves

BEFORE YOU GO ON . . .

1 How did the vigilance committees help fugitive slaves?

2 Why did fugitive slaves learn "Follow the Drinking Gourd"?

HOW ABOUT YOU?

• What do you think it would have been like to travel at night, following the North Star?

Review and Practice

Reread "The Train to Freedom." Then look at a section under one of the article's subheadings. In your notebook, list the main ideas and details of that section. Then summarize the section in your own words. Below is a model showing the main idea and details of the section entitled "The Underground Railroad."

The Underground Railroad

Main Idea: The Underground Railroad helped slaves escape.

Details: It was not really underground or a railroad.

A network of people secretly supported it.

Fugitive slaves were called "passengers."

Runaways rested in places called "stations."

People who led the slaves were called "conductors."

Levi Coffin and Harriet Tubman were conductors.

Now, without looking at your summary, explain the section to a partner. Try to use some of these words: *fugitive, network, runaway, shelter.*

Cotton plant ▶

144

Imagine that you are a conductor on the Underground Railroad. You are helping a group of fugitive slaves travel north to the Ohio River. You are traveling at night, so that the darkness will help to hide you. You are making your trip during the winter, when rivers freeze and become easier to cross. You know how to find the Big Dipper and the North Star, telling you which way is north. You also know where to find stations and people who will help you.

In your notebook, write a journal entry about a day in your journey. Tell what happens on that day and how you feel about it.

DISCUSSION

Discuss in pairs or small groups.

1. The writer calls Harriet Tubman a hero. There are other heroes in the article. In what ways were the fugitive slaves, the "stationmasters," and the abolitionists also heroic?

2. Some slaves didn't try to escape when they had the chance. Why do you think they didn't?

3. Do you think it is important for people today to know about the Underground Railroad? Why or why not?

4. Do you know of other groups of people who have taken risks and faced challenges to achieve freedom? Who are they? What did they do?

Personal Narrative

"Five New Words at a Time" is a personal narrative told by Yu-Lan, an immigrant girl from China. She describes her fear of not understanding people at her new school in the United States. With her mother's help, she faces the challenge of learning English.

FIVE NEW WORDS AT A TIME

"Five New Words at a Time" by Yu-Lan (Mary) Ying, originally published in *The New York Times*, March 6, 1993. Reprinted by permission of *The New York Times*.

Yu-Lan (Mary) Ying

My family came to America in 1985. No one spoke a word of English. In school, I was in an English as a Second Language class with other foreign-born children. My class was so overcrowded that it was impossible for the teacher to teach English properly. I **dreaded** going to school each morning because of the fear of not understanding what people were saying and the fear of being laughed at.

At that time, my mother, Tai-Chih, worked part time in a Chinese restaurant from late afternoon till late in the night. It was her unfamiliarity with the English language that forced her to work in a Chinese-speaking environment. Although her job exhausted her, my mother still woke up early in the morning to cook breakfast for my brother and me. Like a hen guarding her chicks, she never **neglected** us because of her **fatigue**.

---

dreaded, was afraid of; feared
neglected, did not take care of
fatigue, tiredness; exhaustion

146

So it was not surprising that very soon my mother noticed something was troubling me. When I said nothing was wrong, my mother answered, "You are my daughter. When something is bothering you, I feel it too." The pain and care in her moon-shaped eyes made me burst into the tears I had held back for so long. I explained to her the fear I had of going to school. "Learning English is not impossible," my mother said. She cheerfully suggested that the two of us work together to learn the language at home with books. The **confidence** and **determination** my mother had were **admirable** because English was as new to her as it was to me.

That afternoon I saw my mother in a different light as she waited for me by the school fence. Although she was the shortest of all the mothers there, her face with her welcoming smile and big, black eyes was the most promising. The afternoon sun shone brightly on her long, black hair creating an **aura** that distinguished her from others.

My mother and I immediately began reading together and memorizing five new words a day. My mother with her encouraging attitude made the routine fun and interesting. The fact that she was sacrificing her resting time before going to work so that I could learn English made me see the strength she possessed. It made me admire my mother even more.

---

confidence, belief in yourself
determination, strong desire to do something; resolve
admirable, worthy; deserving respect
aura, light that seems to come from a person

BEFORE YOU GO ON . . .

1 Why was Yu-Lan afraid to go to school?

2 What did her mother suggest to help Yu-Lan learn English?

HOW ABOUT YOU?
- Have you ever felt like Yu-Lan? What was your experience?

Very soon, I began to comprehend what everyone was saying and people could understand me. The person solely responsible for my accomplishment and happiness was my mother. The reading also helped my mother learn English so that she was able to pass the postal entrance exam.

It has been seven years since that reading experience with my mother. She is now forty-three and in her second year at college. My brother and I have a strong sense of who we are because of the strong values my mother established for herself and her children. My admiration and **gratitude** for her are endless. That is why my mother is truly the guiding light of my life.

---

gratitude, thankfulness; appreciation

About the Author

Yu-Lan (Mary) Ying

Yu-Lan (Mary) Ying received a degree in chemical engineering from Massachusetts Institute of Technology in 1998. She is currently a medical student.

BEFORE YOU GO ON . . .

1 How did Yu-Lan's mother benefit from reading with Yu-Lan?

2 Why do Yu-Lan and her brother have a strong sense of who they are?

HOW ABOUT YOU?

- Are you grateful to someone who has helped you overcome a difficulty? Explain.

Link the Readings

Both texts in Part 1 are about people who took risks and faced challenges. Reread "Five New Words at a Time," and think about "The Train to Freedom." Copy the chart into your notebook and complete it.

Title of Selection	Genre	Fiction or Nonfiction	Risk or Challenge	Result
"The Train to Freedom"				
"Five New Words at a Time"				

DISCUSSION

Discuss in pairs or small groups.

1. Think about how strong fugitive slaves had to be in order to travel on the Underground Railroad. In what ways were they strong in both mind and body? In what ways is Yu-Lan's mother strong in both mind and body?

2. Sometimes it is easier to take risks or to face challenges with the help and encouragement of other people. In "The Train to Freedom" and "Five New Words at a Time," who received help? Who gave help? Do you think the people who gave help gained anything from the experience? Explain.

3. Fugitive slaves who managed to escape to freedom had to make new lives for themselves in new places, much like immigrants such as Yu-Lan and her family. What challenges do you think former slaves faced in beginning new lives as free people?

Connect to Writing

GRAMMAR

Using Prepositions and Prepositional Phrases

Prepositions are words that tell where, in what direction, and when. Look at the chart.

Where	In What Direction	When
at the hotel	**down** the hall	**before** you begin
in the North	**across** the river	**in** your life
by the fence	**toward** Canada	**after** that

A **prepositional phrase** is a preposition + an object.

preposition object **on** the wall	preposition object **across** the wide river
preposition object **in** her hotel room	preposition object **during** our English class

Practice

Write these sentences in your notebook. Circle the preposition in each sentence. Then underline the prepositional phrase.

Example: Many families were separated (during) their trip.

1. Fugitive slaves traveled across deep rivers.
2. As a slave, Harriet Tubman worked in the fields.
3. Harriet Tubman helped slaves escape to the free North.
4. Harriet Tubman worked on the Underground Railroad.
5. Yu-Lan's mother cooked breakfast early in the morning.
6. Yu-Lan's mother worked in a Chinese restaurant.

SKILLS FOR WRITING

Writing Interview Questions and Responses

Here are some ideas for writing interview questions and responses.

- Remember to ask *wh-* questions (who, what, where, when, why).

- If you don't understand something, ask the person to repeat or explain. Write the person's answers, using his or her exact words.

- Read the model. Then answer the questions that follow.

Kevin D. Ascher

I interviewed my mother about a challenge she faced.

Kevin: When did you go to Tibet?

Mom: Fifteen years ago, after my two-year stay in China.

Kevin: Why was this a challenging experience for you?

Mom: I had no knowledge of the Tibetan language, and only a basic knowledge of Mandarin Chinese. I went alone. I thought I could get lost, or hurt, or sick. I wondered if I would have trouble traveling or finding places to stay.

Kevin: How did you communicate with people there?

Mom: I stayed the first two nights at a Western-style hotel where people spoke English. After that, I moved to a hotel where they didn't speak English. I used my Mandarin Chinese and body language.

Kevin: Did you have a good time?

Mom: Yes! It was the adventure of a lifetime.

---

1. Who is the interviewer? Who is being interviewed?
2. What kind of questions does the interviewer ask?
3. How is the interview format different from the paragraph format?

WRITING ASSIGNMENT

Interview Questions

You will write questions for an interview and record the responses of the person you interview.

1. **Read** Look at the model on page 151. Think of someone to interview. The person should be someone who has faced a challenge.

Writing Strategy: **Wh-** *Question Chart*

A *wh-* question chart can help you brainstorm interview questions. Look at the chart used by the writer of the interview questions and responses on page 151. Then answer the questions that follow.

Challenge: Trip to Tibet

Who:	*Who did you go with?*
What:	*What were some problems you experienced?*
Where:	*Where did you stay?*
When:	*When did you go to Tibet?*
Why:	*Why was this a challenging experience for you?*
How:	*How did you communicate with people there?* *How long did you stay in Tibet?*

1. Which of these questions did the writer ask?
2. Why do you think he didn't ask the other questions?

---

2. **Make a chart** Make a *wh-* question chart in your notebook. Write as many questions as you can. Then copy the questions that you most want to ask on a new notebook page. Leave space under each question for the person's answer.

3. **Interview** Interview the person. Record his or her responses to your questions.

4. **Write** Write and edit your final draft.

EDITING CHECKLIST

Did you . . .

▶ ask *wh-* questions?

▶ use correct interview format?

▶ record the exact words of the person you interviewed?

▶ use prepositions and prepositional phrases correctly?

PART
REVIEW 1

Check Your Knowledge

Language Development

1. How did you skim for main ideas in the texts in Part 1? What did you find out about each text by using this strategy?

2. Give an example of a preposition and a prepositional phrase.

3. What kind of questions do you ask when you conduct an interview?

4. Give a friend two tips for writing interview questions.

Academic Content

1. What new social studies vocabulary did you learn in Part 1? What do the words mean?

2. Who were some of the famous "conductors" on the Underground Railroad? What did you learn about them?

3. What information was hidden in the song "Follow the Drinking Gourd"?

Side door to basement of Graue Mill in Oak Brook, Illinois, believed by historians to have been an Underground Railroad station ◄

Prepare to Read

OBJECTIVES

LANGUAGE DEVELOPMENT

Reading:
- Vocabulary building: *Context, dictionary skills*
- Reading strategy: *Analyzing text structure*
- Text types: *Play, science article*
- Literary element: *Stage directions*

Writing:
- Dialogue
- Making notes

Listening/Speaking:
- Dialogue
- Discussion

Grammar:
- Contractions and apostrophes

Viewing/Representing:
- Illustrations, text format

ACADEMIC CONTENT
- Science vocabulary
- Physical effects of stress
- Fine arts: *Drama*

BACKGROUND

The Little Prince: The Play is a play based on a well-known novel by Antoine de Saint-Exupéry, a French author and airplane pilot. It is the story of someone who learns some important lessons.

The text of plays consists mostly of dialogue between the characters. Characters' names appear next to the lines of dialogue they speak. The text also contains directions to the actors and to the stage crew, usually in parentheses. Here is an example of stage directions: (*LITTLE PRINCE approaches the rose bush.*).

Make connections Read this excerpt from the play. As you read, imagine you are watching the play on the stage.

> **LITTLE PRINCE:** Shall we begin?
> **FOX:** Tomorrow. Meet me right here.
> **LITTLE PRINCE:** Tomorrow?
> **FOX:** Tomorrow.
> (*LITTLE PRINCE exits. Lights change. LITTLE PRINCE reenters.*)

Answer the questions.
1. How can you tell that this is a play?
2. Who are the characters?
3. What are the stage directions?

LEARN KEY WORDS

awkward
essential
ferociously
invisible
monotonous
tamed
unique

VOCABULARY

Read these sentences. Use the context to figure out the meaning of the **red** words. Use a dictionary to check your answers. Write each word and its meaning in your notebook.

1. After the Little Prince said hello to the Rose, there was an **awkward** silence. Neither of them knew what to say next.
2. Food, water, air, and shelter are **essential** for all animals.
3. The man was frightened when the dog growled **ferociously**.
4. Air is **invisible**, but we know it's there because we can breathe.
5. Listening to the same song again and again is **monotonous**.
6. The trainer **tamed** the lion, and it became as gentle as a kitten.
7. People are not all alike. Each individual is **unique**.

READING STRATEGY

Analyzing Text Structure

Analyzing the **structure** of a **text** can help you determine what kind of text you are reading. It can also help set your purpose for reading. Poems, stories, and plays all look different.

- **Stories** are written in paragraphs. Dialogue is enclosed within quotation marks.

- **Poems** are usually written line by line rather than in paragraphs. Punctuation doesn't always follow the same rules in poetry as it does for other types of text.

- **Plays** are mainly dialogue. The dialogue has the speakers' names, followed by colons, and then the words the speaker says. Stage directions are usually in parentheses, for example: (*Lights dim, music fades, LITTLE PRINCE exits left.*).

Preview the play excerpt, looking carefully at characters' names and stage directions. How does the text's structure show you that this is a play? What is your purpose for reading the play?

from The Little Prince: The Play

Rick Cummins and John Scoullar

FOX: Good morning.

LITTLE PRINCE (*stops crying, looks around*): Good morning.

FOX (*scampers across to a tree*): I'm right here under the apple tree.

LITTLE PRINCE: Who are you? You're very pretty to look at. (*LITTLE PRINCE starts to approach FOX. FOX scampers away nervously. . . .*)

FOX: I'm a fox.

LITTLE PRINCE: Will you come play with me? I'm so unhappy. (*. . . LITTLE PRINCE moves toward him. FOX growls.*)

FOX: Play with you—I can't play with you!

LITTLE PRINCE: Why not?

---

scampers, runs with short, quick steps

156

FOX: Because—because—I'm not tamed— and you're a—one of them.

LITTLE PRINCE: Them?

(. . . *FOX scampers away again.*)

FOX: The ones . . . with the guns. The hunters. (*FOX scampers nervously.*) Yeah, you're one of those hunters . . . oh, sure, you don't look dangerous cause you're little. But how can I be sure it's not a trap. Very clever. No, no, as things are, I'd better just—(*FOX begins to scamper off. LITTLE PRINCE stops FOX from leaving. . . .*)

LITTLE PRINCE: But I don't have a gun! (*FOX stops and looks as LITTLE PRINCE opens his arms wide to display no concealed weapon.*) See.

FOX (*looking around*): Then you'd better watch out for them, too. (*He keeps his distance throughout the scene.*)

LITTLE PRINCE: What does that mean "tamed"?

FOX: You don't live around here, do you?

LITTLE PRINCE: What does that mean "tamed"?

FOX: What are you looking for?

LITTLE PRINCE: I was looking for men.

FOX: Men—Brrr! Grr. They have guns and they hunt. It's very disturbing!

LITTLE PRINCE: Oh. . . .

FOX: Are you looking for chickens?

LITTLE PRINCE: What?

FOX: Chickens.

LITTLE PRINCE: No. I was looking for men.

---

concealed, hidden

FOX: Oh, that's right.

LITTLE PRINCE: What does that mean "tamed"?

FOX (*sighs*): Boy, you don't let go of a question, do you? It's an act too often neglected. It means . . . to **establish ties**.

LITTLE PRINCE: To establish ties?

FOX: Yeah . . . see, to me you're just another little boy just like a hundred thousand other little boys and I have no need of you. And you—well, have no need of me. To you, I'm nothing more than a fox like a hundred thousand other foxes.

LITTLE PRINCE: Oh, I see.

FOX: But if you tamed me—to me you'd be unique in all the world. And to you, I'd be unique in all the world. Then—we'd need each other.

---

establish ties, become friends; become important to each other

LITTLE PRINCE: I'm beginning to understand. There was a flower—a rose.

FOX: Like the ones on that wall down the road?

LITTLE PRINCE (*nods sadly*): I think she tried to tame me.

FOX: It's possible. On Earth one sees all sorts of things.

LITTLE PRINCE: Oh, but this wasn't on Earth.

FOX: Wasn't on Earth?

LITTLE PRINCE: No.

FOX: Some other planet, maybe?

LITTLE PRINCE: Yes.

FOX: Right—are there hunters on that planet?

LITTLE PRINCE: No.

FOX: Hmm . . . Are there chickens?

LITTLE PRINCE: No.

FOX: Well, nothing's perfect.

LITTLE PRINCE: No.

FOX: No. (*Pause.*) My life, you know . . . it's well, it's . . . I hunt chickens. Men hunt me. All the chickens are alike. All the men are alike. It's—very monotonous.

LITTLE PRINCE: What?

FOX: Well see, **I search me out a chicken**—hey, a fella's got to eat. But then, the hunters, they chase me through the woods and down the hills until I have to

---

I search me out a chicken, I try to find a chicken for myself

dive into a hole to hide from them until they give up. Every day it's pretty much the same old thing. (*Yawn.*) Search, run, hide. Sometimes I sit down in that hole for hours just thinking.

LITTLE PRINCE: About what?

FOX: About—what it might be like if it was—different. If someday, someone came along—someone without a gun. Someone whose footsteps would make me excited instead of sending me **scurrying** away. Someone who would— (*He looks at LITTLE PRINCE.*) . . . tame me.

LITTLE PRINCE: I'd like to, really, but I don't have much time. I have so many things to understand.

FOX: You only understand the things you tame. Men have no time to understand anything, so they have no friends. If you want to understand—if you want a friend—you've got to tame me.

LITTLE PRINCE: What must I do to tame you?

FOX: You must be very **patient**. I'm still a wild animal, after all. First, we'll sit down together in the grass. (*FOX indicates LITTLE PRINCE to sit further and further away until they are quite far apart.*) Then I'll look at you out of the corner of my eye and you will say nothing. Words are the source of misunderstanding. But every day we will sit a little closer. Day after day.

---

scurrying, running away quickly
patient, able to wait for something without getting angry

LITTLE PRINCE: Shall we begin?

FOX: Tomorrow. Meet me right here.

LITTLE PRINCE: Tomorrow?

FOX: Tomorrow.

(*LITTLE PRINCE exits. Lights change. LITTLE PRINCE reenters.*)

LITTLE PRINCE: Good morning!
(*LITTLE PRINCE catches FOX asleep and is much too close. FOX **reflexively** growls ferociously and **snaps**, catching LITTLE PRINCE's hand in his mouth. After a moment he slowly **extracts** it, **battling with his own nature**. LITTLE PRINCE rubs his hand. FOX puts distance between them.*)

FOX: Say—uh—Don't *do* that!

LITTLE PRINCE: What is it that—

FOX: Like I said, my experience with people has not been all that good. You okay there?

LITTLE PRINCE: I think so.

---

reflexively, automatically; without thinking about it
snaps, bites
extracts, takes out
battling with his own nature, fighting something inside himself; experiencing conflicting feelings

---

BEFORE YOU GO ON . . .

1 What does the Fox think about when he is in his foxhole?

2 Why does the Fox growl ferociously when the Little Prince approaches him the first time?

HOW ABOUT YOU?

• What do you think about the Fox's plan for becoming friends with the Little Prince?

FOX: You know, maybe this just isn't such a good idea, maybe—

LITTLE PRINCE: No, no really, I'm fine. But—what is it that I did?

FOX: WELL! You can't just stroll up for a visit anytime at all. If you're gonna tame me, you've got to come at the same time every day. Didn't I mention that? (*LITTLE PRINCE shakes his head.*) It's got to be a ritual. If you come at the same time every day, then every day about an hour before you're due, I'll start getting excited. Rituals are very important. Especially in taming.

LITTLE PRINCE: I think I understand.

FOX: Do you think? You see those grain fields down yonder. Well, **wheat** is of no use to me. I mean, the **wheatfields have nothing to say to me** and that is sad. But you have hair that is the color of gold. Now if you tamed me, the wheat, which is also golden, will bring me back the thought of you and I shall love to listen to the wind in the wheat.

---

wheat, a grain used to make bread
wheatfields have nothing to say to me, I don't care about wheatfields

LITTLE PRINCE: I understand now. Shall we begin?

FOX: Ready when you are.

BOTH: One, two, three, go!

(*. . . They proceed to perform a ritual representing the taming process. . . . They circle around . . . and then back . . . passing the point where they started. They come to rest at a distance from each other. . . . LITTLE PRINCE and FOX face the audience, occasionally looking at each other out of the corner of their eyes, awkwardly trying to maintain a silence.*)

LITTLE PRINCE: I was thinking, did you ever—

FOX: Shh. Not a word! (*Disappointed at their **failure**, they repeat circle action, **saluting** as they go, with lighting changes, arriving a little closer to one another. Again they stand facing the audience in awkward silence.*) Nice scarf.

LITTLE PRINCE: Nice tail.

FOX: It was a gift from my mother. (*Repeat same actions, saluting again, circling more hopefully. Their movements **accelerate**. . . . They extend their pattern to make a figure-eight past each other. Then they **do-si-do** around each other. They finally arrive face-to-face.*)

---

failure, something that does not succeed
saluting, waving "hello" or "goodbye"
accelerate, speed up
do-si-do, walk around each other with their backs to each other (dance step)

LITTLE PRINCE: Are you tame now?

FOX: I don't know. Let's find out. (*Slowly, LITTLE PRINCE reaches to touch him. FOX tries to fight off urge to growl and finally LITTLE PRINCE pets him. FOX doesn't growl. In fact, much to his surprise, he **nuzzles** LITTLE PRINCE.*) YES! I'm tame! I'm finally tame. (*They sit. FOX nuzzles like a puppy dog as lights fade.*) (*. . . After a brief pause, lights come up again. LITTLE PRINCE is sitting, **absorbed** in his own thoughts as FOX is moving around playfully.*)

FOX: Let's see. Yesterday we explored the hills, and the day before, the forest. Shall we dance today, or shall we chase each other through the wheatfields?

LITTLE PRINCE: No, I don't think so. (*LITTLE PRINCE sits down in the grass.*)

FOX: I know. Let's play hide and seek. I'll hide. I've had lots of practice.

LITTLE PRINCE: Not today.

---

nuzzles, rubs with the nose
absorbed, totally focused on or interested in something

BEFORE YOU GO ON . . .

1 Why will the wheat remind the Fox of the Little Prince?

2 How can the Little Prince tell that the Fox is tame?

HOW ABOUT YOU?

• What rituals do you participate in? Explain.

FOX (*nestles down next to him. After a moment*): You are thinking about your rose again. Listen to me. Go now and take another look at the wall full of roses and you'll understand.

LITTLE PRINCE: Understand what?

FOX: You'll see. Then come back to say goodbye to me.

LITTLE PRINCE: Goodbye? What do you mean?

FOX: Just go. And when you come back I will tell you a secret.
(*LITTLE PRINCE walks to the wall of roses. They are giggling. He sees them . . . and sighs.*)

LITTLE PRINCE: You are not at all like my rose. As yet you are nothing. No one has tamed you and you have tamed no one. You are beautiful, but you are empty.

One could not die for you. You are like my fox when I first met him—like a hundred thousand other foxes. But now I have tamed him, and made him my friend and now he is unique in all the world. An ordinary **passerby** would think that my rose looked just like you— the rose that belongs to me. But she is more important than all the hundreds of you other . . . roses because it is *she* that I have watered; because it is *she* that I have sheltered behind the screen; because it is for *her* that I have killed the caterpillars except the two or three we saved to become butterflies, because it is *she* that I have listened to when she asked questions, or grumbled, or even sometimes when she said nothing, because she is *my* rose.
(*. . . LITTLE PRINCE returns to FOX.*)

---

giggling, laughing

passerby, a stranger who walks by

LITTLE PRINCE: The time has come for me to go.

FOX: Ah . . . I shall cry.

LITTLE PRINCE: But I never wished you harm—you wanted me to tame you.

FOX: Yes, that is so.

LITTLE PRINCE: Then it has done you no good at all.

FOX: It has done me good—because of the wheatfields. I will always remember you when I see them because they are the color of your hair. One runs the risk of **weeping** a little, when one allows himself to be tamed.

LITTLE PRINCE: Goodbye.

FOX: Goodbye. And now here is my secret. A very simple secret. Repeat after me so you will always remember it. It is only with the heart that one can see **rightly**. (*FOX lays his hand on LITTLE PRINCE's heart.*)

LITTLE PRINCE: It is only with the heart that one can see rightly. (*LITTLE PRINCE lays his hand on FOX's heart.*)

FOX: What is essential is invisible to the eye. (*FOX touches LITTLE PRINCE's eye.*)

LITTLE PRINCE: What is essential is invisible to the eye.

---

weeping, crying
rightly, truly; correctly

About the Authors

Antoine de Saint-Exupéry
Rick Cummins and John Scoullar

French author and pilot Antoine de Saint-Exupéry (1900–1944) wrote the novel *The Little Prince* in 1943. Saint-Exupéry's novel was made into a play by Rick Cummins and John Scoullar.

Rick Cummins (left) composes music for plays, musicals, and other productions.

John Scoullar (right) has written lyrics for musical performances, children's songs, books, and rock videos.

BEFORE YOU GO ON . . .

1 Why does the Fox say it is good that he was tamed?

2 What is the Fox's secret?

HOW ABOUT YOU?

• How would you feel if a close friend had to move far away?

Review and Practice

The excerpt you read from *The Little Prince: The Play* tells a story. What happens in the beginning, the middle, and the end of the story? Copy this chart into your notebook. Use it to record the events in the play excerpt. You can use the text in the first box as a model.

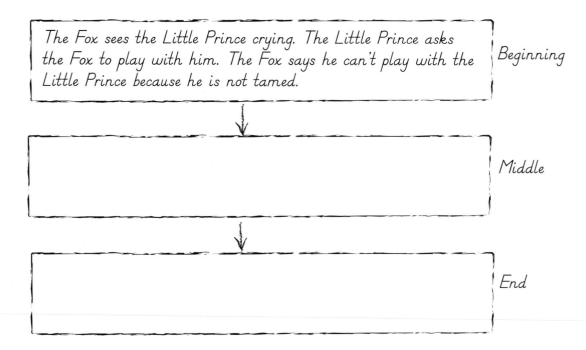

The Fox sees the Little Prince crying. The Little Prince asks the Fox to play with him. The Fox says he can't play with the Little Prince because he is not tamed.

Beginning

Middle

End

Use your chart to tell the story to a classmate or family member.

EXTENSION

The Fox teaches the Little Prince an important lesson. His words are in the first column of the chart. Reread the excerpt from *The Little Prince: The Play* and think about the meaning of the Fox's words. Then copy the chart into your notebook and complete it.

What the Fox Says	In My Own Words	Why I Agree or Disagree
"It is only with the heart that one can see rightly."		
"What is essential is invisible to the eye."		

DISCUSSION

Discuss in pairs or small groups.

1. Why does the Fox want the Little Prince to tame him?
2. What is the difference between the roses in the wall and the Little Prince's rose?
3. In the Extension section, you discussed the sentence, "What is essential is invisible to the eye." What are some things you consider essential? Why?

*This is an article that gives you information about performance **anxiety** and tips for public speaking or performance. Notice how the format of this article is different from the format of the play. Look at the tips. How does the format make them easier to read?*

Performance Anxiety

Stress is the reaction of your mind and body to situations that seem dangerous or disturbing. A "stressor" is something that causes this reaction. There are many kinds of stressors. A test in school, an argument, a **threatening** situation, or an **injury** might cause stress.

For many people, speaking or performing in public causes stress. Think about a time when you had to stand in front of your class or another audience, and speak or perform. How did you feel?

If you are like many of us, you felt stress. There are physical causes for this feeling. The body responds to stressful situations by pumping a chemical called adrenaline into your bloodstream. Adrenaline increases your heartbeat, giving you more energy and preparing your body to respond quickly. These changes are often called the "fight-or-flight" response, because they prepare you to either run or stay and fight the stressor. This response is present in all animals, so that they can fight or run away from danger. Athletes today use their own adrenaline response to run faster and play better.

Today, most of our stressors are not things we fight or run away from. Actors don't run off the stage or

---

anxiety, a feeling of worry or nervousness
threatening, causing fear or alarm
injury, a cut, burn, or other harm to your body

Adrenaline pumps through this tennis player's body, helping him play well. ▶

stay to fight with the audience! But our bodies still react to stress. We **release** adrenaline. Our breathing and heartbeat are faster. Our hands feel cold as blood is pumped away from these areas to other places. And less blood flows to our **digestive system**. We might feel "butterflies" in our stomach when we are frightened or nervous.

In modern life, these feelings are not always good or useful. Luckily, there are ways to reduce them. In the case of performance anxiety, or "stage fright" —a term taken from the theater—there are other specific things you can do to reduce stress. Breathing deeply can help relax you. This will help your flow of blood and oxygen return to normal. Here are some other tips you can use to calm your mind and body before a performance.

▲ Students watch a school play rehearsal.

1 **First of all, prepare.** You will be more relaxed if you feel ready. If you are giving a speech, practice in front of a mirror. Practice on tape. Give the speech to your dog, cat, or baby sister. It helps to practice in front of a small audience before you face a large one. It's also helpful to practice your lines with friends or family members. If you are singing or playing a musical instrument, perform your piece for friends or family. And remember that it's important to come to all the play or concert rehearsals.

2 **Don't try to guess what your audience is thinking.** If you see a man with his eyes closed, for example, don't **immediately** think that he is bored. Maybe he is listening and concentrating. Or if you hear people talking, don't **assume** it's because they are not happy with your performance. Maybe they are asking questions about the piece you are performing.

3 **Remember that you have a talent and that you are sharing it.** Think of your audience as wanting to receive what you have to give. Think of your

---

release, let circulate in our bodies
digestive system, the mouth, stomach, intestines, and other organs that help people or animals eat, process food, and get rid of waste
immediately, right away; without waiting
assume, believe that something is true

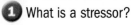

BEFORE YOU GO ON . . .

1 What is a stressor?

2 What happens to your body when you feel stress?

HOW ABOUT YOU?
- What are some things that cause you to be anxious?

performance as a gift from you to your listeners, and do your best. Try looking at different people in the audience and imagine that you are performing just for them. Make eye contact. Speak to them. Sing to them. Play for them.

4 **Allow yourself to enjoy what you are doing!** Feel your emotions, and enjoy the excitement of your performance. Don't let mistakes **interfere** with your enjoyment. If you forgive your own mistakes and keep going when you make them, the audience will probably forgive them, too! Often an audience doesn't care as much about **perfection** as about the feeling the performer can **project**. If you make a mistake, forget it, keep going, and keep your heart in your performance!

---

interfere, interrupt, stop, or get in the way of
perfection, faultlessness; excellence
project, communicate to the audience

BEFORE YOU GO ON . . .

1 Where should you look when you are performing?

2 What should you do if you are giving a speech and you make a mistake?

HOW ABOUT YOU?

- Which tip do you think is the most helpful? Why?

Actors try to feel the emotions of their characters. ▶

Link the Readings

REFLECTION

The Little Prince: The Play and "Performance Anxiety" both deal with taking risks or facing challenges. Reread "Performance Anxiety" and think about *The Little Prince: The Play*. Then copy the chart into your notebook and complete it.

Title	Genre	Challenge/Risk
From *The Little Prince: The Play*		*Allowing yourself to make friends with someone can be risky.*
"Performance Anxiety"		

DISCUSSION

Discuss in pairs or small groups.

1. In what ways is making friends risky? How is performing for an audience risky?

2. Discuss how actors can overcome "stage fright." Have you ever had stage fright? Were you able to overcome it? If so, how?

Connect to Writing

GRAMMAR

Contractions

A **contraction** is two words combined into one with an **apostrophe** ('). An apostrophe takes the place of a missing letter or letters.

I **did not** understand the question.	I **didn't** understand the question.

Contractions are almost always used in spoken English, informal writing, and written dialogues. When writing is more formal, contractions are generally avoided.

Here are some common contractions.

Contractions with *be*

I am	**I'm**	we are	**we're**
you are	**you're**	they are	**they're**
he is	**he's**	there is	**there's**
she is	**she's**	it is	**it's**

Contractions with *will*

I will	**I'll**
You will	**you'll**
She will	**she'll**

Contractions with *would*

I would	**I'd**
You would	**you'd**
She would	**she'd**

Negative contractions

is not	**isn't**	were not	**weren't**
are not	**aren't**	did not	**didn't**
do not	**don't**	had not	**hadn't**
does not	**doesn't**	will not	**won't**
has not	**hasn't**	can not	**can't**
have not	**haven't**	could not	**couldn't**
was not	**wasn't**	would not	**wouldn't**

Practice

Write six sentences in your notebook using contractions of the following: *they are, does not, you will, will not, you would, would not.*

SKILLS FOR WRITING

Writing Dialogue

Dialogue is conversation in a book, play, interview, or movie. In the writing assignment for Part 1 on page 152, you wrote dialogue in your interview. In the excerpt from *The Little Prince: The Play,* you saw how dialogue is written in a play.

Stories and personal narratives can also include dialogue. In these types of writing, a writer places **quotation marks** (" ") before and after the exact words that a character speaks. The spoken words, also called a quotation, begin with a capital letter and end with a comma, a period, a question mark, or an exclamation point. The punctuation goes inside the closing quotation mark. When one character finishes speaking and another one begins, the writer begins a new paragraph.

> The Fox eyed the Little Prince carefully and asked, "What are you looking for?"
>
> "I was looking for men," replied the Little Prince.
>
> "Men!" cried the Fox. "They have guns and they hunt." Then he added, "It's very disturbing!"

Read the model. Notice how dialogue is written. Then answer the questions.

1. Identify the spoken words, or the quotations, in the story excerpt.
2. How many times does the speaker change?
3. Identify the punctuation marks that come before the closing quotation marks in each quotation.

WRITING ASSIGNMENT

Dialogue

You will write a short dialogue that might appear in a story. The dialogue should be between two students who are planning a performance of the play *The Little Prince*.

1. **Read** Look at the example of story dialogue on page 171 to recall how dialogue is written in a story.

Writing Strategy: Making Notes

Before you write your dialogue, you can organize what the people will say by making notes. Try to summarize the main ideas of the dialogue before you write the actual words people say:

> *Linda wants Tom to audition for the play. She thinks he would be good as the Little Prince. Tom is nervous about trying out, and he's not sure that he will do it.*

---

2. **Make notes** In your notebook, make some notes that you can use to get ideas for your dialogue. Try to imagine a conversation between the two people you will be writing about. Think about sentences and/or questions that one person would say and how the other person would answer.

3. **Write** Look at your notes. Use them to write a dialogue as it would be written in a short story.

EDITING CHECKLIST
Did you . . .

▶ write dialogue that sounds like real people speaking?

▶ use contractions correctly?

▶ use quotation marks around the speaker's words?

▶ use commas, periods, and other punctuation correctly?

Check Your Knowledge

Language Development

1. What about the text structure of *The Little Prince: The Play* shows you that it is a play and not a short story?

2. What are some reasons for stage directions in a play?

3. How is dialogue presented in a play? How is it presented in a story or a personal narrative?

4. What is a contraction? What is the purpose of an apostrophe in a contraction? Give an example.

5. How can making notes help you prepare to write a dialogue?

Academic Content

1. What new science vocabulary did you learn in Part 2? What do the words mean?

2. What are some effects of anxiety on your body? How can it be useful?

3. What are some ways to reduce the effects of stress?

Put It All Together

OBJECTIVES

Integrate Skills
- Listening/
  Speaking:
  TV commercial
- Writing:
  *Biographical
  narrative*

Investigate
Themes
- Projects
- Further
  reading

TV COMMERCIAL

You will write a TV commercial for a play and present it to the class.

 Think about it Work in small groups. Make a list of plays you have seen or read, or that you know about. Then discuss your list, and choose one play to write about.

The purpose of a commercial is to persuade people to do something—in this case, to see a play. What will persuade people to see your play? List your ideas. Your group may wish to act out a short scene from the play or interview someone who has seen the play and liked it. As a group, decide on the best way to advertise your play.

2 Organize Work together to write your commercial. Which students will present the different parts? For example, some students might act out a scene. Others who have seen the play can give their opinions. Discuss the order in which students will present their information.
Prepare any costumes or props you may need.

3 Practice Practice your commercial with your group. Memorize your lines.

4 Present and evaluate Present your commercial to the class. Did your commercial persuade your classmates to see the play? If so, what made it effective? If not, where was it weak?

SPEAKING TIPS

- Communicate your belief in what you are saying, so the audience will believe it, too.
- Have fun. The more your viewers enjoy the commercial, the more they will want to see the play.

LISTENING TIP

Evaluate not only what presenters are saying, but also how they are saying it. Often a speaker's manner and body language can be more or less persuasive than the content of what he/she is saying.

174

BIOGRAPHICAL NARRATIVE

In a biographical narrative, the writer tells a story about another person's life. Usually, the writer describes the person's actions and feelings concerning a conflict or problem.

A biographical narrative should include the following:

- a person the story is about—the subject of the story
- third-person point of view (the pronoun *he* or *she*)
- information that answers the *wh-* questions
- chronological organization of events
- the person's actions and feelings concerning the conflict or problem

You will interview a person about a risk he or she took, and then write a biographical narrative about the experience. The risk might be about a time the person tried to do something new and learned something about himself or herself as a result. Use the model essay, information from your interview, and the following steps to help you.

 Prewrite Choose someone to interview. The person can be a family member, friend, or classmate who has taken a risk and learned something from the experience. Use a *wh-*question chart to write questions for your interview. Possible questions might include:

- Who took the risk?
- Where and when did the situation happen?
- What risk did he or she take?
- Why did he or she take it?
- What happened and what did he or she learn?

Interview the person. Write his or her answers to your questions.

WRITING TIPS

- When you write a biographical narrative, remember to use the third-person point of view (the pronoun *he* or *she*).
- Use quotation marks if you want to include dialogue.

Before you write a first draft of your narrative, read the model. Notice the characteristics of a biographical narrative.

Jennifer Rosario

Students don't usually pick their high school. However, students with parents in the military can choose between the public school or a school on the military base. My friend Crystal faced this decision last year. Her choice involved taking a risk. "I can stay in a school on the base where I'm comfortable," she told me. "Or I can make a change and go to public school."

In August, Crystal asked me to help her pick a school. We compared the size, student population, dress code, academic programs, and extracurricular activities of the schools. The school on the base had lots of pluses. It was smaller and less competitive. It was also safer because Crystal had friends there.

After careful thought, Crystal made a decision that surprised everyone. She enrolled in the public school. "Even though it's more competitive, stricter, and bigger, I wanted a challenge," she said. "Also, it offers a program that would let me graduate in three years. The high school on the base doesn't have that." Crystal took the risk because she realized that challenging herself in a new school was more important than being comfortable in a familiar one.

Subject of the story

Third-person point of view

Uses time phrases to present events in chronological order

Narrator reveals Crystal's feelings about her decision.

2 **Draft** Use the model and the information from your interview to write your biographical narrative.

- Start your narrative in an interesting way, so your audience will want to keep reading your story.
- Describe the risk the person took and how he or she felt about it.
- Consider using dialogue in your narrative to make it more realistic and interesting.
- Conclude your narrative by describing what the person learned from the experience.

3 **Edit** Work in pairs. Trade papers and read each other's narratives. Use the editing checklist to evaluate each other's work.

EDITING CHECKLIST

Did you . . .

- ▶ use the pronoun *he* or *she* to tell the story?
- ▶ use prepositions and prepositional phrases correctly?
- ▶ use contractions correctly?
- ▶ use quotation marks and commas to quote the person's exact words?

4 **Revise** Revise your narrative. Add details and correct mistakes, if necessary.

5 **Publish** Share your narrative with your teacher and classmates.

PROJECTS

Work in pairs or small groups. Choose one of these projects.

1 With a partner, research songs that are part of our African-American heritage, such as slave songs or spirituals. Learn to sing the songs or find a recording. Report to your class on the history of the songs and play or perform them for your classmates.

2 With a partner or small group, write a short play about someone taking a risk or facing a challenge. It can be about a person from history, such as Harriet Tubman, or about others who were involved in the Underground Railroad. Use *The Little Prince* as a model. Then perform your play for the class.

3 Work with classmates to stage a production of *The Little Prince*. If possible, make scenery and costumes. Practice your play and perform it for other students. You could also perform the play as readers theatre. For readers theatre, the characters don't follow the stage directions or wear costumes. They just read the lines with expression.

4 Find out more about a job that involves risks, such as being a firefighter, police officer, paramedic, journalist, documentary filmmaker, or construction worker. Once you have found out facts about the job and what it requires, write a "help wanted ad" for it. Be sure to include the job requirements and explain some of the risks involved.

5 Create a travel brochure for a "challenging" vacation adventure. Would you enjoy the challenge of diving hundreds of feet below the surface of the ocean or exploring an unknown cave? Find out more about such an adventure and make a travel brochure. You can include photographs from magazines, actual brochures, or the Internet.

Further Reading

To find out more about the theme of this unit, choose from these reading suggestions.

Robin Hood, **Howard Pyle** Robin Hood, an English folk hero, has been the subject of countless stories and songs since the 1300s. This book describes his adventures in Sherwood Forest, where he risks his life robbing from the rich to give to the poor.

Robinson Crusoe, **Daniel Defoe** Robinson Crusoe is at sea when a storm leaves him shipwrecked on a deserted island. He is completely alone for almost thirty years. His challenge is to survive on his own and make a home for himself. Will hard work, courage, and determination be enough for him to succeed?

Harriet Tubman, **George Sullivan** This biography describes Harriet Tubman's extraordinary life from birth to death. It tells of her experiences as a slave, her escape from slavery, her tireless work on the Underground Railroad, and her years as a spy for the Union army.

The Boy in the Alamo, **Margaret Cousins** When his brother sets out to fight at the Alamo, young Billy Campbell follows him. Through Billy's eyes, we experience the events of that famous battle. We also learn of the heroes who gave their lives fighting to free Texas from Mexico.

Esperanza Rising, **Pam Muñoz Ryan** When Esperanza's father dies, so does the life she knows and loves. She and her mother leave Mexico to live and work in a migrant labor camp in California. Esperanza is miserable in her new life. But when her mother becomes ill, Esperanza learns that she can do far more than she ever knew.

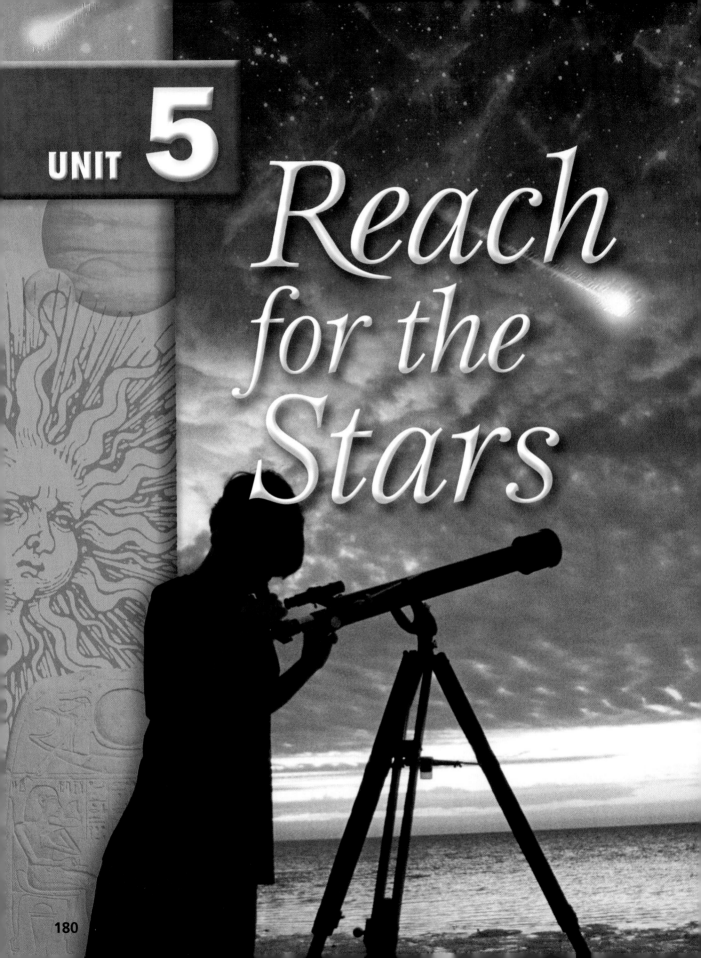

Reach for the Stars

PART 1

- "Earth and the Milky Way"
- *The Starry Night* (painting),
  Vincent van Gogh
- "On van Gogh's *Starry Night*,"
  Martha Staid
- "Escape at Bedtime,"
  Robert Louis Stevenson

PART 2

- "The Ten Chinese Suns"
- "Re"
- "Why the Sun Is So High in the Heavens"
- "Solar Eclipses"

What do you see when you look at the night sky? Do you see millions of twinkling lights? Do you see the shapes of animals or objects in the stars? Do you see the sad face of the moon staring back at you? In this unit, you will find out what some scientists, artists, and poets see in the night sky.

In Part 1, you will read an article about Earth, the sun, and our place in the universe. Then you will view a starry night through the eyes of a famous artist. You will also read poems that offer other views of the stars.

In Part 2, you will read some myths that people created long ago to explain the world around them. Finally, you will read an article about solar eclipses and learn a safe way to view an eclipse.

Prepare to Read

OBJECTIVES

LANGUAGE DEVELOPMENT

Reading:
- Vocabulary building: *Dictionary skills*
- Reading strategy: *Using a K-W-L-H chart*
- Text types: *Science article, poems*
- Literary element: *Personification*

Writing:
- Research: *Internet, print*
- Using note cards
- Research report
- Comparing and contrasting

Listening/Speaking:
- Sharing information

Grammar:
- Comparative and superlative adjectives

Viewing/Representing:
- Paintings, star map, photographs

ACADEMIC CONTENT
- Science vocabulary
- The solar system and the Milky Way galaxy
- Vincent van Gogh

BACKGROUND

"Earth and the Milky Way" is a science article. It gives information about Earth, our solar system, and the Milky Way galaxy.

Make connections Look at the photograph of the moon and discuss the questions.

1. Did you see the moon last night? Was it a full moon? A crescent?
2. What other objects can you see in the sky at night?
3. Is it important to study space? Is it important for people to travel in space? Why or why not?

LEARN KEY WORDS

asteroid
comets
extinct
gas
gravity
meteorite

VOCABULARY

Read the sentences. Look up each **red** word in a dictionary. Notice the parts of each dictionary entry: the pronunciation, the part of speech, and the meaning. An entry may include a sample sentence to show how the word is used. It also may include information about the word's history. For each key word, find the dictionary meaning that matches the way it is used in the sentence in your textbook. Write the word and its meaning in your notebook.

or•bit (ôr'bĭt) *v.* to travel in a circle in space around a much larger object, such as Earth or the sun: *Venus orbits the sun once every 225 Earth days.* [from the Latin *orbita*, meaning "track"]

1. An **asteroid** circles the sun just as the planets do.
2. Some **comets** are bright enough to see without a telescope.
3. The biggest volcano in the solar system is now **extinct**.
4. The scientist could smell the dangerous **gas** in the air after the accident, although he couldn't see it.
5. Astronauts wear heavy shoes on the moon because the moon's **gravity** isn't as strong as the gravity of Earth.
6. A piece of rock or dust that travels through space and lands on Earth is called a **meteorite**.

READING STRATEGY

Using a K-W-L-H Chart

A K-W-L-H chart is useful when you are reading a text. It can help you use your background knowledge about a topic, ask questions that will help you read, record information, and think about how you learned. It can also help you establish your purpose for reading the text.

K—What I Already **K**now	**W**—What I **W**ant to Know	**L**—What I **L**earned	**H**—**H**ow I Learned

1. In the *K* column, write what you already know about the topic.
2. In the *W* column, write what you want to know about the topic.
3. Wait until after you read the text to fill in the *L* and *H* columns.

EARTH
AND THE MILKY WAY

From Earth, the stars appear as tiny dots in the sky. In fact, each star in the sky is an **enormous** glowing ball of gas, like our sun.

A huge, organized collection of stars is called a galaxy. Our solar system is located in the galaxy called the Milky Way. Our sun is one of more than 100 billion stars located in the Milky Way.

---

enormous, very, very big

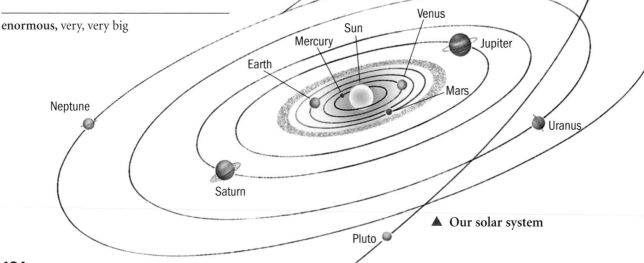

▲ Our solar system

184

Our Solar System

Our solar system consists of the sun, nine planets and their moons, an asteroid belt, and many comets and meteors. The sun is the center of our solar system. The planets, more than sixty-one moons, asteroids, comets, and meteorites, all orbit the sun.

The Sun

Our sun is a medium-sized star. It is a huge, spinning ball of hot gas that lights up Earth and provides us with heat. It is 149,680,000 kilometers (93,026,724 mi.) from Earth.

Scientists determine the temperature of the sun by measuring how much heat and light it **emits**. The sun's **core** can reach 5,500,000 to 15,000,000°C (10,000,000 to 27,000,000°F). The outer **atmosphere** of the sun is also extremely hot—830,000 to 1,000,000°C (1,500,000 to 2,000,000°F). Sunspots are areas of gas on the sun that are cooler than the gases around them. In photographs, sunspots look darker than other parts of the sun because cooler gases don't give off as much light as hotter gases.

Since the sun is the closest star to Earth, astronomers study it to understand the **nature** of stars in general. They use special instruments to analyze the light from the sun, its effect on Earth's climate, the sun's magnetic field, solar wind, and many other solar **phenomena**.

▲ Sun spots appear as dark areas on the sun's surface.

---

emits, sends out; gives off
core, center part
atmosphere, the mix of gases that surrounds a star or planet
nature, qualities; characteristics
phenomena, facts or events that can be seen

BEFORE YOU GO ON . . .

1 What is a galaxy? What is the name of Earth's galaxy?
2 What does the sun emit?

HOW ABOUT YOU?
- What do you know about the planets in our solar system?

The Planets

Planets are bodies (gaseous or solid) that orbit stars. They are not hot enough to glow, but they shine if they reflect light from a sun. A sun is any star that has planets orbiting it. Both stars and planets can be seen glowing at night. The nine planets that orbit our sun are Mercury, Venus, Earth, Mars, Jupiter, Saturn, Uranus, Neptune, and Pluto.

The four planets closest to the sun—Mercury, Venus, Earth, and Mars—are called the inner planets. The inner planets are small and have solid, rocky surfaces. Thousands of pieces of rock and metal, called asteroids, orbit the sun between Mars and Jupiter. They separate the inner planets from the outer planets. The five outer planets are Jupiter, Saturn, Uranus, Neptune, and Pluto. Four planets— Jupiter, Saturn, Uranus, and Neptune—are called the gas giants because they are much larger than Earth and do not have solid surfaces. These four planets have rings. Pluto is smaller than Earth and, like Earth, it has a solid surface and no rings.

From Earth, we can see five other planets without a telescope: Mercury, Venus, Mars, Jupiter, and Saturn. We need a telescope to see Uranus, Neptune, and Pluto. These nine planets may not be the only planets. Scientists are still finding new bodies that orbit our sun.

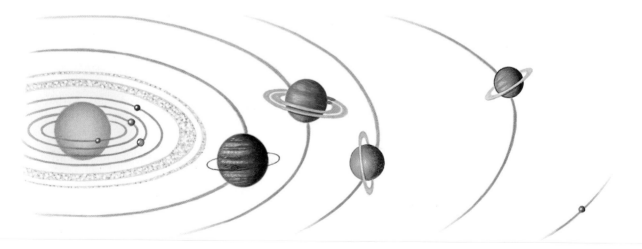

▲ The inner planets, asteroid belt, and outer planets of our solar system

▲ Comet Hale-Bopp

Asteroids, Comets, and Meteoroids

There are other objects smaller than planets and moons that also orbit the sun. They include asteroids, comets, and meteoroids.

Asteroids are rocky or metallic objects in many sizes and shapes. Most asteroids orbit the sun in a belt, or group, between the orbits of Mars and Jupiter. This area of the solar system is called the asteroid belt. Astronomers have discovered more than 10,000 asteroids.

Comets are large pieces of ice and dust that orbit the sun. When a comet travels near the sun, the energy in the sunlight changes the ice into gas. Gas and dust form a tail, which can be hundreds of millions of kilometers long.

Meteoroids are dust particles or bits of rock that travel through space. They usually come from comets or asteroids. When a meteoroid enters Earth's atmosphere, it burns up and produces a streak of light in the sky, called a meteor. Large meteoroids may not burn up completely. Meteoroids that hit a planet or moon are called meteorites. Meteorites caused the **craters** on the moon.

▲ Chunk of stony iron meteorite that landed on Earth

___
craters, round holes in a surface made by something that has hit it

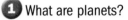

BEFORE YOU GO ON . . .

1 What are planets?

2 What planets are visible from Earth without a telescope?

HOW ABOUT YOU?
- Would you like to be an astronomer? Why or why not?

The Stars

Most stars are in pairs or in **clusters**. The force of gravity holds these pairs or clusters together. Two stars that are locked together in orbit are called a binary star system. About half of all stars are in binary star systems. Larger groups of stars, or clusters, are also joined together by their gravitational pull.

Patterns of stars in the sky are called constellations. Constellations are different from star pairs or clusters because the connection among the stars is only **visual**. There is no gravitational or orbital connection, and distances between the stars in the constellation may be very **great**.

---

clusters, groups of things of the same kind that are very close together
visual, relating to sight
great, large

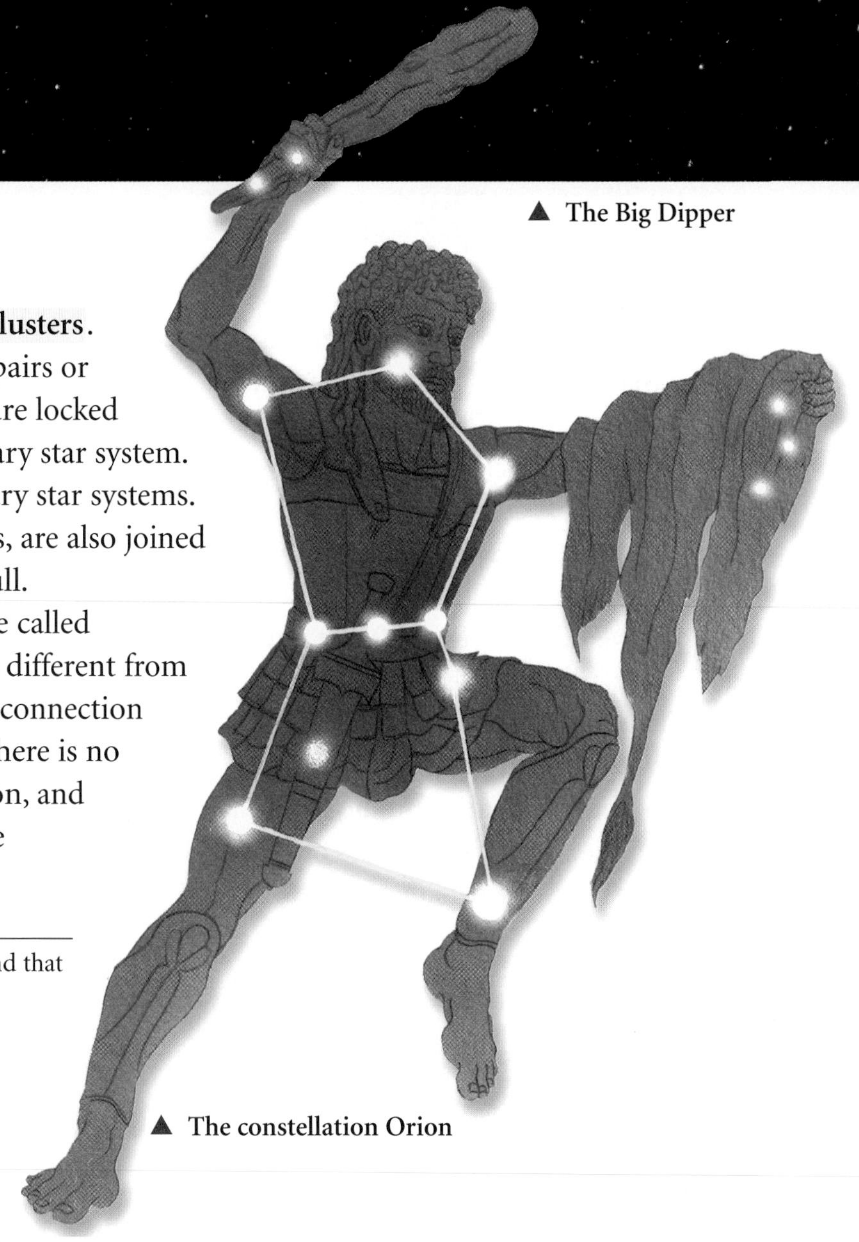

▲ The Big Dipper

▲ The constellation Orion

Constellations of the zodiac ▶

[star map illustration of the constellations of the southern sky, with labels including Aquarius, Balena, Pisces Austrinus, Phœnix, Capricornus, Grus, Indus, Taurus, Fluvius, Orion, Lepus, Dorado, Hydrus, Apous, Camel., Corona Aust., Pavo, Canis maior, Gemini, Sagittarius, Ara, Triangulum, Argo Navis, Canicula, Cancer, Scorpius, Lepus, Centaurus, Hydra, Crater, Leo, Libra, Corvus, Virgo]

There are eighty-eight recognized constellations. **In ancient times**, people called twelve of these constellations the zodiac. *Zodiac* is the Greek word for "animals," and most of the constellations in the zodiac are named after animals. Learning the constellations is a way to **become familiar with** the stars in the same way that people have been doing for thousands of years.

Star maps help astronomers locate stars in the same way that land maps help us find our way around Earth. Astronomers divide the sky into a grid similar to the **latitude** and **longitude** grid used on land maps. Astronomers use the star grid system to chart the positions of stars.

---

in ancient times, very long ago
become familiar with, get to know; learn about
latitude, distance north or south of the equator
longitude, distance east or west of the meridian (imaginary line from the top of the world to the bottom that divides east and west)

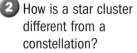

BEFORE YOU GO ON . . .

1 What is a binary star system?

2 How is a star cluster different from a constellation?

HOW ABOUT YOU?

• Do you know the names of any other stars or constellations? If so, which?

189

Solar System Facts

Jupiter

The biggest planet in the solar system is Jupiter. All the other planets could fit inside it. On Jupiter, there is a huge storm that has already lasted for hundreds of years. It is about 28,000 kilometers (17,000 mi.) long and 14,000 kilometers (9,000 mi.) wide. It is called the Great Red Spot, and it is so big that two Earth-sized planets could fit inside it.

▲ Jupiter

Jupiter has rings, but they are faint, dark, and narrow, so they are not easy to see. Jupiter's rings are made up of tiny bits of rock and dust that orbit the planet. The dust is created as a result of tiny meteorites crashing into Jupiter's moons.

The biggest moon in the solar system is Ganymede, a moon of Jupiter. Ganymede has a **diameter** of 5,262 kilometers (3,280 mi.). It is bigger than the planet Pluto or Mercury. Its diameter is about one third that of Earth.

Saturn

Saturn is the second biggest planet in the solar system. Like Jupiter, Saturn has a thick atmosphere, composed mostly of hydrogen and helium. Although Saturn has clouds and storms, they are much milder than those on Jupiter. Saturn is the only planet that is less dense than water. Saturn's famous rings are much larger and brighter than the rings of other planets. Unlike Jupiter's rings, Saturn's rings are made up of chunks of rocks and ice.

---

diameter, length of a line that divides a circle in half

Venus

Venus is closest in size to Earth. Venus's diameter is 95 percent of Earth's diameter, and its **mass** is 82 percent of Earth's mass. Venus is the planet that **passes** closest to Earth in its orbit. It is roughly 39,200,000 kilometers (24,588,879 mi.) from Earth at its closest **approach**. Venus is the hottest planet, with temperatures up to 480°C (896°F).

▲ Venus

Mars

The biggest volcano in the solar system, Olympus Mons, is on Mars. It is 27 kilometers (17 mi.) tall and over 520 kilometers (320 mi.) across. It **erupted** about 200 years ago. It is now believed to be extinct.

▲ Mars

Pluto

The smallest planet is Pluto. Pluto is smaller than our moon. It is the coldest planet and has temperatures as low as −238°C (−396°F).

---

mass, the amount of material in something
passes, goes across or around something
approach, movement toward or near
erupted, exploded and sent off fire and smoke

▲ Pluto

◀ Saturn

BEFORE YOU GO ON . . .

1 What is the largest planet in the solar system? What is the smallest?

2 What is the Great Red Spot?

HOW ABOUT YOU?

• Which planets would you like to learn more about? Why?

Review and Practice

Reread "Earth and the Milky Way." Then copy the chart into your notebook. Write one fact about each topic in the chart. If there is a word in parentheses, use that word in your fact. Use the fact about asteroids as a model.

Topic	Fact
Asteroids	*Asteroids orbit the sun.*
Milky Way galaxy	
Comets	
Meteoroid (*meteorite*)	
Stars	
Pluto (*visible*)	
Venus	
Mars (*enormous*)	
Sun (*emits*)	

◀ Hubble Space Telescope

192

EXTENSION

1. Look at the K-W-L-H chart that you started to fill in before you read the article. Now fill in the *L* column with what you learned, and the *H* column with how you learned it. Compare your charts in pairs.

2. Put the following items in order of their size, from smallest to largest: solar system, Milky Way, Pluto, Ganymede, the sun, Earth, meteoroid.

3. Use information in the article to write riddles. For example: *What am I? I am made of the sun, nine planets, an asteroid belt, and comets and meteors. (Answer: the solar system)* Ask each other your riddles.

DISCUSSION

Discuss in pairs or small groups.

1. What was the most interesting thing you learned about the solar system? Would you like to become an astronaut and travel to another planet? Why or why not?

2. Compare and contrast the inner and outer planets.

3. Explain how a star grid system is used.

▲ Relative sizes of planets compared with the sun

Poetry and Paintings

In this section, you will read about a famous painter. You will also look at his painting The Starry Night *and one of his self-portraits. Then you will read two poems about stars.*

Vincent van Gogh was born in 1853 in Holland. He became a painter when he was in his twenties and moved to France in 1886. Van Gogh spent the last years of his life in the south of France, painting landscapes and people. He suffered from mental illness and was confined at various times to mental hospitals, where he continued to paint until his death in 1890. Van Gogh sold only one painting during his lifetime. Today a van Gogh painting is worth millions of dollars. One of van Gogh's most famous paintings is *The Starry Night*.

▲ Vincent van Gogh's painting *The Starry Night*

Self-portrait of
Vincent van Gogh ▶

This poem is about van Gogh's
The Starry Night.

On van Gogh's
Starry Night

The sky is **crack'd** with **radiance** and seems,
To speak in tones too cosmic and too low,
For us to hear, and yet the **canvas teems**
With messages we guess but never know.

It speaks of balance **'tween** the sky and land,
The one **ablaze**, the other soft and dim,
And hints the presence of a master hand,
Protecting those who sleep and trust in Him.

The stars are soft, as if they're viewed through tears,
Melting into a **solemn**, saddened glow,
A **testament** to hard and troubled years,
Yet overall the starlight serves to show,

Amid the darkest **trials** of this world,
Is beauty found in galaxies bright-swirl'd.

Martha Staid

---

crack'd, cracked
radiance, brightness
canvas teems with, the painting is full of
'tween, between
ablaze, on fire
solemn, very serious or sad
testament, proof
trials, difficulties or hardships

BEFORE YOU GO ON . . .

1. What does the poem say about the stars in the painting?
2. According to the poem, was the painter happy? Explain.

HOW ABOUT YOU?

- Do you like the painting? The poem? Why or why not?

195

Escape at Bedtime

The lights from the **parlour** and kitchen shone out
Through the **blinds** and the windows and bars;
And high overhead and all moving about,
There were thousands of millions of stars.
There **ne'er** were such thousands of leaves on a tree,
Nor of people in church or the Park,
As the crowds of the stars that looked down upon me,
And that **glittered** and winked in the dark.
The Dog, and the **Plough**, and the Hunter, and all,
And the star of the **sailor**, and Mars,
These shown in the sky, and the pail by the wall
Would be half full of water and stars.
They saw me at last, and they chased me with cries,
And they soon had me packed into bed;
But the glory kept shining and bright in my eyes,
And the stars going round in my head.

Robert Louis Stevenson

LITERARY ELEMENT

Personification is giving human traits to animals, plants, or objects. Here is an example: *As the crowds of the stars that looked down upon me.* Find another example of personification in the poem.

---

parlour, living room
blinds, objects that cover windows
ne'er, never
glittered, were very shiny
plough, a farmer's tool
sailor, a person who works on a ship

BEFORE YOU GO ON . . .

1 What are the Dog, the Plough, and the Hunter?

2 How does the person in the poem feel about the stars?

HOW ABOUT YOU?
- How do you feel when you look at stars?

196

Link the Readings

Reread the poems, and look at the painting and the star map again. Think about the texts you read in Part 1. Copy the chart into your notebook and complete it.

Title of Selection	Genre	Purpose of Selection	What I Liked about It
"Earth and the Milky Way"			
The Starry Night			
"On van Gogh's *Starry Night*"			
"Escape at Bedtime"	*poem*		

DISCUSSION

Discuss in pairs or small groups.

1. Summarize a section of "Earth and the Milky Way." Include only the most important ideas in that section.

2. Look at van Gogh's self-portrait on page 195. How is his painting of himself similar to *The Starry Night*?

3. Find an example of personification in "On van Gogh's *Starry Night*." Is there anything in the science text that makes you think of personification?

4. Would you rather talk to a scientist who studies stars or a poet who writes about them? Why?

Connect to Writing

GRAMMAR

Comparative and Superlative Adjectives

Use **comparative adjectives** to compare two people, places, or things. Use **superlative adjectives** to compare three or more people, places, or things.

> Comparative: Asteroids are **smaller than** planets.
> Superlative: Jupiter is **the largest** planet in our solar system.

Form the comparative and superlative of most one-syllable and some two-syllable adjectives like this:

Adjective	Comparative	Superlative
small	small**er than**	**the** small**est**
hot	hot**ter than**	**the** hot**test**
easy	eas**ier than**	**the** eas**iest**

Use **more** or **most** to form the comparative and superlative of most adjectives with two or more syllables like this:

Adjective	Comparative	Superlative
beautiful	**more** beautiful **than**	**the most** beautiful

Some adjectives have irregular comparative and superlative forms:

Irregular Adjective	Comparative	Superlative
good	**better than**	**the best**
far	**farther than**	**the farthest**

Practice
Write sentences using these words and comparative adjectives.

1. solar system / small / Milky Way
2. comets / long / meteorites
3. Earth / heavy / Venus

Write sentences using these words and superlative adjectives.

1. Pluto / far / planet from the sun
2. Earth / beautiful / planet
3. Olympus Mons / big / volcano

198

SKILLS FOR WRITING

Using the Internet to Do Research Reports

The purpose of a research report is to give the reader factual information about a topic. Before you write a report, you need to find information. One place to look for information is on the Internet. However, not everything you find on the Internet is correct. Anyone can put information on the Internet, so be careful. Check several sources to be sure your facts are correct.

Follow these steps to do your research on the Internet.

1. Go to a search engine. At the search engine, type in the topic of your report and click "search."

2. You will see links to websites about your topic. Click the links of the websites that you want to read. Find facts about your topic and write notes for your report.

Look at these two Internet screens. Then work with a partner. Ask and answer the questions.

Back Forward Reload Home Search
Search for: Search Tips
	Jupiter		Search	
Browse Our Directory
Arts   Health   News
Movies   Fitness   Media
TV   Medicine   Weather
Music   Nutrition   Top Stories

▲ Screen 1

Back Forward Reload Home Search
Website Matches
1. **Jupiter** update—learn the newest discoveries and take a quiz about **Jupiter** http://www.jpd.planets.com/**jupiter/** More sites about: planets and Jupiter
2. Out of this world—view great photos of Jupiter http://www.outofthis world.com/photos/planets/**jupiter** More sites about: solar system and Jupiter

▲ Screen 2

1. Look at Screen 1. What information is the researcher looking for?
2. Look at Screen 2. What is the name of the site that has photographs?
3. Which website has a quiz about Jupiter?

WRITING ASSIGNMENT

Research Report

You will write a research report comparing and contrasting two or more planets, using the Internet (and other sources) to research your topic.

1. **Read** Reread the article "Earth and the Milky Way" to review facts about the planets. Which planets provide interesting points to compare and contrast? Choose planets to write about.

Writing Strategy: Note Cards

It is important to keep track of where you get information. In a formal report, article, or book, writers include a bibliography—a list of sources, or references, that follows a specific format. In shorter, more informal reports, a bibliography might not be required, but a writer must be able to say what sources were used. Note cards can help you keep track of your sources.

As you read different sources, take notes. Write important facts or ideas on cards. On the back of each card, write the source.

- For Internet articles, list the author, the title of the article, and the website.
- For books, list the title, the author, the publisher, the publication date, and the page number.
- For magazines, list the author, the title of the article, the name of the magazine, the date or issue, and the page number.
- For newspapers, list the reporter, the title of the article, the name of the newspaper, the page and column, and the date.

2. **Do your research** Use the Internet (and other sources) to find information for your report. Skim several sources. Then go back and carefully read those that relate most closely to your topic.

3. **Write** Use the information you found to write your report.

Check Your Knowledge

Language Development

1. What information about words can you find in a dictionary?

2. How can a K-W-L-H chart help you focus on a text?

3. What is an example of personification?

4. How do you form comparative adjectives? Superlative adjectives? Write a sentence using each one.

5. What is the purpose of a research report? Why is it important to take notes as you do your research and include information about the sources you used?

Academic Content

1. What new science vocabulary did you learn in Part 1? What do the words mean?

2. What are the names of the planets in our solar system? What are asteroids, comets, and meteoroids?

3. Who is Vincent van Gogh?

4. Describe how you do research on the Internet.

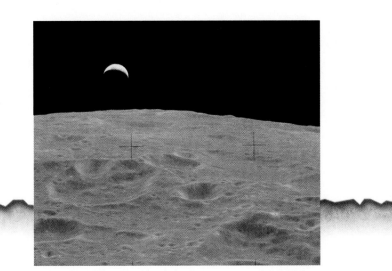

▲ The moon's surface with Earth (partially lit) in background sky

201

OBJECTIVES

BACKGROUND

Myths are very old fictional stories that are usually part of the oral tradition. Myths were often created to explain things about the natural world. The myths you will read in this section come from three different cultures, and all deal with the sun and its heat and power. "The Ten Chinese Suns" is from China and explains how ten suns became just one. The second myth, "Re," is about the Egyptian sun god and creator. The third myth, "Why the Sun Is So High in the Heavens," is from the Huichol culture. The Huichols, who live in the Western Sierra Madre Mountains in Mexico, explain why the sun once lived close to Earth and why it moved away.

Make connections Take turns sharing myths that you know with your classmates.

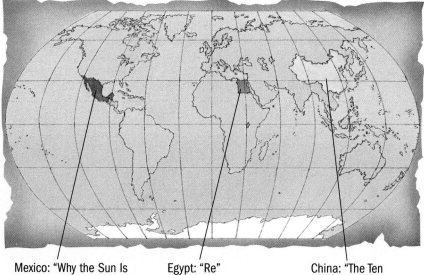

Mexico: "Why the Sun Is So High in the Heavens"　　Egypt: "Re"　　China: "The Ten Chinese Suns"

202

beloved
condemned
content
disobedient
mortals
unbearable

VOCABULARY

Read these sentences. Use the context to figure out the meaning of the **red** words. Use a dictionary to check your answers. Write each word and its meaning in your notebook.

1. He cried when his **beloved** daughter left the family house and moved to an apartment.
2. The judge **condemned** the criminal to five years in prison.
3. She has a good job, a nice family, good friends, and good health—so she is very **content**.
4. Although Sam usually does what his parents tell him to do, sometimes he is **disobedient**.
5. Many myths are about gods or goddesses who are forced to live the lives of ordinary **mortals** here on Earth.
6. The heat was **unbearable**, so we went swimming in the river.

READING STRATEGY

Identifying Causes and Effects

Whether your purpose for reading is to be entertained or informed, **identifying causes and effects** as you read can help you better understand a text. Most fiction and nonfiction texts tell about events that happen. Why an event happens is a cause. What happens as a result of a cause is an effect. The words *so* and *because* often signal causes and effects:

        cause   effect
People wanted to explain the natural world, **so** they made up myths.

    effect   cause
People told myths **because** they wanted to explain the natural world.

As you read the myths and the article in Part 2, look for signal words to help you identify causes and effects.

Myths

As you read each myth, look at the story events closely to identify causes and effects. Keep in mind that words such as because *and* so *often signal causes and effects.*

The Ten Chinese Suns

CHINESE MYTH

Chinese people once believed that there were ten suns that appeared **in turn** in the sky during the Chinese ten-day week. Each day the ten suns traveled with their mother, the goddess Xi He, to the Valley of the Light in the East. There, Xi He washed her children in the lake and put them in the branches of an enormous mulberry tree called fu-sang. Then, from the tree, one of the ten suns moved off into the sky for the one-day journey to Mount Yen-Tzu in the Far West.

---

in turn, one after the other

The ten suns became tired of this **routine**, so they all decided to appear at the same time. The combined heat of the ten suns made life on Earth unbearable. To prevent the destruction of Earth, the emperor Yao asked Di Jun, the father of the ten suns, to persuade his children to appear **one at a time**.

Di Jun could not persuade the ten suns to appear one at a time. So Di Jun sent the archer, Yi, armed with a magic bow and ten arrows to frighten the disobedient suns. But instead of using the arrows to frighten the suns, Yi shot nine of them, leaving only the sun that we see today. Di Jun was so angry with Yi for killing nine of his children that he condemned Yi to live as an ordinary mortal on Earth.

---

routine, the normal or usual way of doing things
one at a time, separately

Yi with his magic bow ▶

BEFORE YOU GO ON . . .

1 What routine did the ten suns have?

2 What did the ten suns do to make life on Earth unbearable?

HOW ABOUT YOU?

- Because the ten suns didn't follow the routine, it caused a problem for people on Earth. Can you think of other examples where there was a problem when someone didn't follow a routine?

Re

EGYPTIAN MYTH

Re was known as the sun god and the creator of the world in ancient Egypt. He could change his form, or appearance, so he was portrayed in different ways in ancient Egyptian art. Artists usually portrayed Re with a hawk's head, wearing a fiery disk like the sun on his head. Around the disk was a **cobra**-goddess, representing his power to bring death. In the Underworld, the place where spirits of the dead lived, Re changed form and had a ram's head. In this form, Re had power over Osiris, god of the Underworld.

Re's main job was to bring the sun across the sky and the Underworld. His other job was to protect the **pharaohs** of Egypt.

The Egyptians believed Re created the world like this: Re had two children, Shu and Tefnut, who became the atmosphere and clouds. They had more children, Geb and Nut, who became Earth and the stars. They in turn had two sons, Seth and Osiris. One day Re wept, and humans were created from his tears. Re also created the four seasons for the Nile, a very important river in Egypt and the longest river in the world.

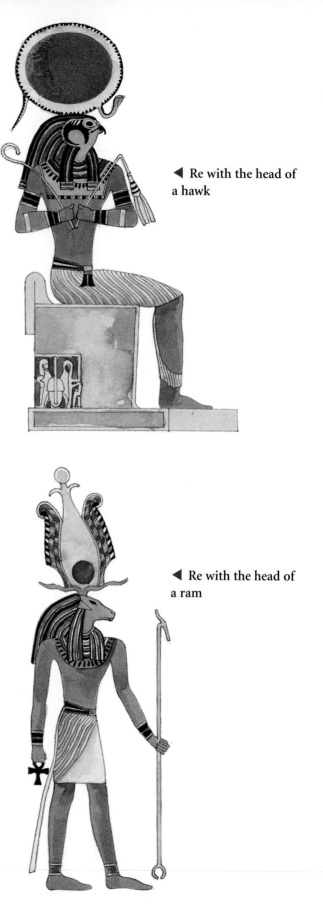

◄ Re with the head of a hawk

◄ Re with the head of a ram

---

cobra, a poisonous snake
pharaohs, rulers of ancient Egypt

WHY THE SUN IS SO HIGH IN THE HEAVENS

MEXICAN MYTH

Long ago, the Huichols lived in the mountains. They farmed on the **rugged slopes** and hunted wild turkeys.

The Huichol people loved and respected the sun, for a god lived within it.

"What shall we call the sun?" they asked.

"I know," a little boy said. "The call of the wild turkey that greets the rising sun is beautiful. The turkey is like the sun, for it has been given to help us live."

The wild turkey's call went "Shoé-pi-tou-tou-tou." So the Huichols called the sun Tou.

The Huichols would have been content with their way of life except for one problem. Their beloved sun was too close to Earth. Tou was **lonely** and wanted to be near the people of Earth.

Because the sun was so close, Earth became hotter and hotter. People, animals, and crops were being burned up. The people wanted Tou to go high into the sky, but Tou **could not bear** to live far from Earth.

The boy who named the sun had an idea. He said, "I'll go with you, Tou, if you will travel higher in the sky."

So Tou agreed. Tou rose higher in the sky, taking the boy with him. In a little while, Tou stopped and asked the people, "Will this do?"

---

rugged slopes, rocky or dangerous sides of hills or mountains
lonely, unhappy because he was alone
could not bear, found it unbearable; was unable

BEFORE YOU GO ON . . .

1 Describe Re. What did he look like? What were his "jobs"?

2 Why did the Huichol people call the sun Tou?

HOW ABOUT YOU?

• If you had to think of a new name for the sun, what would you call it? Why?

"No," the people replied. "It is still too hot. Go higher."

So Tou rose higher yet in the sky, taking the boy with him. Again he asked, "Is this far enough?" Again the people told him to go even higher, for it was still too hot.

Three more times Tou stopped, and each time the people told him to go higher. On the last time, the people finally said to Tou, "That is just right. You should be just that high in the sky."

The sun was content to remain there. The boy was there too, so the sun didn't feel lonely. The people were content, too, for Earth was no longer burning hot.

Ever since, the sun has remained at just the right distance from Earth. It gives the people pleasant light and warmth instead of burning them up. It helps the plants grow. For these things, the people give the sun thanks and praise.

LITERARY ELEMENT

The *theme* is the central idea, or message, of a work of literature. The themes of "Why the Sun Is So High in the Heavens" and "The Ten Chinese Suns" are similar. In both stories, the sun has to be cooled down so that life on Earth is bearable. The myths share this central idea: We need the sun's light and warmth, but its power can harm us.

BEFORE YOU GO ON . . .

1 Why did the people want Tou to go so high in the sky?

2 How was life better when Tou was at the right distance from Earth?

HOW ABOUT YOU?

● Which myth about the sun did you like the best? Why?

209

Review and Practice

Copy the sentences into your notebook. Which myth does each sentence describe? Write *Chinese, Egyptian,* or *Huichol* after each sentence. Note: Some of the sentences describe more than one myth.

1. Ten suns were reduced to one sun.

2. Earth was too hot because of heat from the sun.

3. The sun god had the head of a hawk.

4. The sun was part of a family of suns and other parts of nature.

5. The sun was lonely without its friends from Earth.

In your notebook, write one sentence that tells how all three myths are alike. Share your sentence with a partner.

▲ Tuthmosis III making offerings to the sun god Ra-Harakhty (*Ra* is an alternative form of *Re.*)

Many myths explain how something—such as an aspect of nature—was created or came to be. Create a story about how something in nature came to be. Your story can be about the sun or anything in nature. Illustrate your story. Then share it with the class.

DISCUSSION

Discuss in pairs or small groups.

1. Why do you think that different peoples created myths about the sun? What did you learn about the people who told these stories?

2. Write one question about the sun that each myth tries to answer. Then compare your questions.

3. Find causes and effects in each myth. How did identifying these causes and effects help you better understand each story?

Apollo, Surya, and Re:
Greek, Indian, and Egyptian
sun gods ▶

211

This article contains facts about what happens when the moon passes between Earth and the sun. This event is called a solar eclipse. Before you read, preview the article and adjust your purpose for reading.

SOLAR ECLIPSES

▲ Sun, moon, and Earth during a solar eclipse

A solar eclipse occurs when the moon passes directly between Earth and the sun, casting a shadow on the surface of the Earth. From Earth, it looks as if the moon has blocked out the light of the sun.

Eclipses may be partial or total. A partial eclipse occurs when the moon hides only part of the sun. A total eclipse occurs when the sun is completely hidden by the moon. Total eclipses of the sun are very **rare**, occurring about once every 360 years in the same location. However, several solar eclipses may occur each year.

In ancient times, people were frightened by solar eclipses because they did not know what was happening. Now eclipses are of great interest to astronomers and to the public. Eclipses provide an opportunity to view the sun's outer atmosphere, the solar corona.

▲ Total solar eclipse

---

rare, unusual; not common

Never look directly at the sun. It can cause **permanent** eye damage or **blindness**. If you have the chance to view a solar eclipse, you can make an eclipse-viewing box to view it safely.

Eclipse-Viewing Box

You will need:

- a long box or tube
- a pair of scissors
- a piece of aluminum foil
- tape
- a pin
- a sheet of white paper

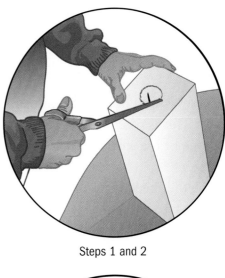

Steps 1 and 2

1. Find or make a long box or tube. The length of the box is important. The longer the box, the bigger the image you will see.

2. Carefully cut a hole in the center of one end of the box.

3. Tape the piece of foil over the hole.

Step 3

---

permanent, lasting for all time
blindness, the condition of being unable to see

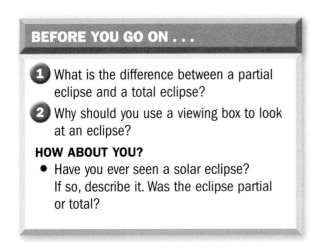

BEFORE YOU GO ON . . .

1. What is the difference between a partial eclipse and a total eclipse?
2. Why should you use a viewing box to look at an eclipse?

HOW ABOUT YOU?

- Have you ever seen a solar eclipse? If so, describe it. Was the eclipse partial or total?

4 Make a small hole in the aluminum foil with the pin. This hole is what the light from the eclipse will go through.

5 Cut a viewing hole in the side of the box. This is where you will see the **image** of the solar eclipse.

6 Tape the sheet of paper inside the end of the box near the viewing **portal**. The paper should be flat against the end that is opposite the pinhole.

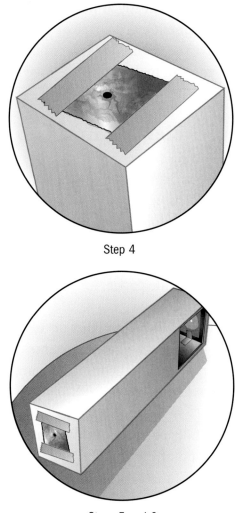

Step 4

Point the end of the box with the pinhole at the sun so that you see a round image on the paper at the other end. If you are having trouble pointing the box at the eclipse, look at the shadow of the box on the ground. Move the box so that the shadow looks like the end of the box (so the sides of the box are not casting a shadow). The round spot of light you see on the paper is a pinhole image of the sun. *Remember: Do not look at the sun! Look only at the image on the paper.*

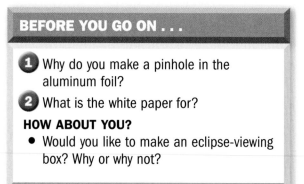

Steps 5 and 6

image, a picture of something
portal, hole for viewing

BEFORE YOU GO ON . . .

1 Why do you make a pinhole in the aluminum foil?

2 What is the white paper for?

HOW ABOUT YOU?

• Would you like to make an eclipse-viewing box? Why or why not?

Link the Readings

Reread "Solar Eclipses" and think about the stories you read in Part 2. Copy the chart into your notebook and complete it.

Title of Selection	Genre	Fiction or Nonfiction	Purpose of Selection	What I Liked about It
"Solar Eclipses"				
"The Ten Chinese Suns"				
"Re"				
"Why the Sun Is So High in the Heavens"				

DISCUSSION

Discuss in pairs or small groups.

1. Imagine that you made an eclipse-viewing box and someone asked you, "What is that box? How do you use it? Why do you need it?" Work with a partner to answer these questions.

2. In "Solar Eclipses," you read the scientific explanation of solar eclipses. How do you think an ancient storyteller might have explained a solar eclipse? Create a myth to explain an eclipse.

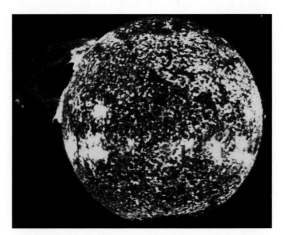

▲ Close-up view of the sun, showing a blast of hot gas

Connect to Writing

GRAMMAR

Using the Passive Voice

A sentence can be in the active voice or the **passive voice**.

> active voice: The sun god **created** the four seasons.
> passive voice: The four seasons **were created** by the sun god.

Use a form of **be + past participle** of the verb to form the passive voice.

> A total eclipse occurs when the sun **is hidden** by the moon.

Use the active voice to focus on the *performer* of an action.

performer	action	receiver
Yi	**shot**	nine of the suns.
Eclipses	**frightened**	ancient people.

Use the passive voice to focus on the *receiver* of an action.

receiver	action	performer
Nine of the suns	**were shot**	by Yi.
Ancient people	**were frightened**	by eclipses.

Use the phrase **by + noun or pronoun** with the passive voice when it is important to know who or what performed the action of the verb.

> The sun was called Re **by the ancient Egyptians**. (important information)

When it is not known or important to say who performed the action, do not use the **by** phrase.

> The sun **was studied** in ancient cultures. (We don't know who studied it.)
> Many soldiers **were killed** in the war. (not important to say who killed them)

Practice

In your notebook, write three sentences using the active voice. Then rewrite the sentences using the passive voice.

SKILLS FOR WRITING

Quoting and Paraphrasing

A **quotation** is a restatement of a person's exact words. When you include a quotation in a report, you must put quotation marks (" ") around the words. When you quote, use the exact punctuation, capitalization, and spelling from the original text.

> Noel Wanner writes, "The word *eclipse* comes from a Greek word meaning abandonment. Quite literally, the eclipse was seen as the sun abandoning the earth."

A **paraphrase** is a restatement of a person's words in your own words. When you write a report, you usually paraphrase ideas. You can often use the word *that* to introduce the idea you are paraphrasing. When you paraphrase, never use the exact words or phrasing of the original text. It's not necessary to use the punctuation, capitalization, or spelling from the original text.

> Noel Wanner writes that the Greek word for *eclipse* means abandonment, and that the Greeks believed the sun was abandoning Earth in an eclipse.

Practice

Copy the sentences into your notebook. Write *Q* next to the sentence if it is a quotation. Write *P* next to the sentence if it is a paraphrase.

1. The Huichols said that their sun was too hot.
2. Noel Wanner stated, "The eclipse was seen as the sun abandoning the earth."
3. The Huichol sun legend starts with the words, "Long ago, the Huichols lived in the mountains."
4. My teacher told me that it's dangerous to look directly at the sun.
5. Scientists say that there are few total eclipses from any one point on Earth.

WRITING ASSIGNMENT

Research Report

You will write a three-paragraph research report, using a variety of sources, about a place where ancient people studied the sun.

1. **Read** Reread the myths on pages 204–209. Think about how the people in these ancient cultures felt about the sun. Then choose one of these cultures or any other ancient culture that studied the sun. You might start by looking up the word *sun*, or the name of a specific culture or country, such as *Huichol* or *Egypt*.

Writing Strategy: Paraphrasing

1. Read your source material several times.
2. Put the source material away. On a note card or piece of paper, write what you learned in your own words.
3. Check your paraphrase with the source material to see if you included all the important information.
4. On the back of the card or paper, record information about your source material. Include the author's name, the page or pages you used, the title of the resource, the date it was created, and where it was created.

---

2. **Paraphrase resource material** Use the steps above to help you paraphrase the information for your report. Remember to use a separate note card or sheet of paper for each of your resources.

3. **Write** Use your note cards or sheets of paper to help you write your research report.

EDITING CHECKLIST

Did you . . .

▶ use paraphrasing to write information in your own words?

▶ use passive and active voices correctly?

▶ use correct punctuation with any quotations you included?

Check Your Knowledge

Language Development

1. What are causes and effects? How does identifying causes and effects help you as you read?

2. What is theme? What theme do two of the myths share?

3. What is paraphrasing? Compare and contrast paraphrasing and quoting.

4. How is the active voice different from the passive voice? Write a sentence using each.

5. How can paraphrasing help you write a research report?

Academic Content

1. What new science vocabulary did you learn in Part 2? What do the words mean?

2. What happens during a solar eclipse? How can you watch a solar eclipse without hurting your eyes?

3. What similarities and/or differences among the three cultures can you see in the three sun myths? How is Re, from the Egyptian legend, different from Tou, from the Huichol legend? Explain two ways in which they are different.

▲ Aztec Temple of the Sun

Put It All Together

OBJECTIVES

Integrate Skills
- Listening/ Speaking: *Research report*
- Writing: *Research report*

Investigate Themes
- Projects
- Further reading

LISTENING and SPEAKING WORKSHOP

RESEARCH REPORT

The first thing to do when preparing a research report is to choose a topic. Then you use a variety of sources to gather, examine, and present information about your topic. Sources might include reference books, biographies, history books, newspapers, magazines, and the Internet.

You will present an oral report to the class about one of the planets in our solar system.

 Think about it Choose a planet from the texts in Unit 5. List all the facts that you know about the planet. Work with other students who chose the same planet. Compare your fact lists and check your facts in your textbook. Find additional facts about the planet in other sources.

 Organize Decide the order in which students will speak and what they will say.

3 **Practice** Practice giving your report in your group. Group members should listen and give suggestions.

 Present and evaluate Present your report to the class. As each group finishes, evaluate the presentation. How might students improve their presentation?

SPEAKING TIPS

Use a visual aid, such as a picture, map, or chart, to illustrate your report.
- Make your visual aid large enough so everyone in the class can see it.
- Don't put too much information on a visual aid. Too many words are difficult for people to read from where they are sitting.
- Keep your eyes and your voice directed at your audience. If you look at the visual aid, people may not be able to hear or understand you.

LISTENING TIPS

As you listen to a report, evaluate the speaker's facts.
- If you aren't sure that a fact is accurate or correct, you can question the speaker's source of information. For example, you might say: "You said that Saturn has sixteen moons. What is your source for that information?"
- Remember to wait until a speaker is finished presenting before asking a question.

WRITING WORKSHOP

RESEARCH REPORT

A written research report is similar to an oral research report, except it is meant to be read, not heard. Your written research report should include the following:

- introductory material that presents your topic and main ideas
- clearly organized information about your topic, gathered from several sources
- facts, details, or examples that explain your topic and support your main ideas
- a list of your sources

You will write a research paper based on material you gather from different sources. You can write about an astronomer, an astronaut, a space mission, or another topic of interest related to this unit. Use the model and the following steps to help you.

1 Prewrite Choose a topic that interests you. Ask yourself, "What do I want to know about my topic?" Write a list of questions about your topic. Use these questions to research and write your report. Each question can be a main idea of your report.

As you do research, use different sources, such as encyclopedias, biographies, science books, magazines, newspapers, and the Internet. Make note cards for your main ideas and important facts. If necessary, review how to make note cards on page 200.

Then organize your cards and write an outline for your report.

WRITING TIPS

Use your questions and note cards to make an outline.

- Put your note cards about the same question together. (If you wrote five questions, you will have five groups of note cards.)
- Write a main idea for each of your questions. Write each main idea after a roman numeral (I, II, III, etc.) in your outline.
- Find supporting details in your note cards for your main ideas. Write each detail after a capital letter (A, B, C, etc.). Indent your details.
- Use visual aids, such as pictures, maps, or charts, to illustrate your research report.

Before you write a first draft of your report, read the following model. Notice the characteristics of a research report.

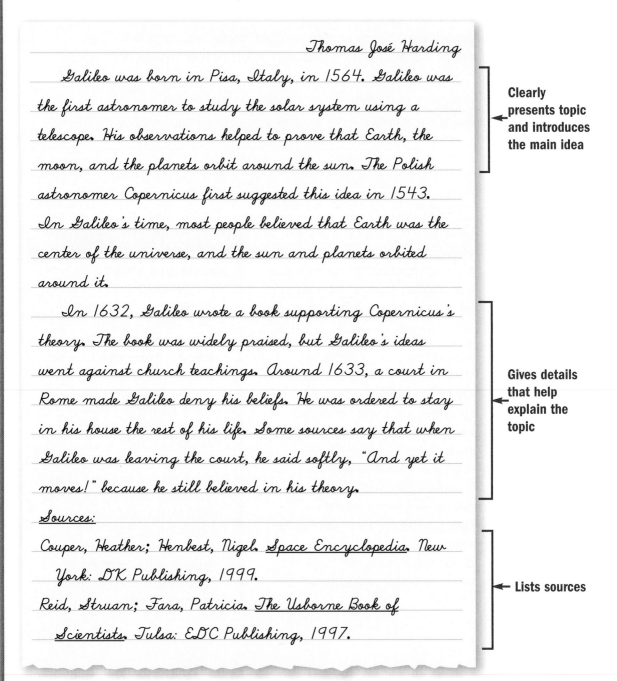

Thomas José Harding

Galileo was born in Pisa, Italy, in 1564. Galileo was the first astronomer to study the solar system using a telescope. His observations helped to prove that Earth, the moon, and the planets orbit around the sun. The Polish astronomer Copernicus first suggested this idea in 1543. In Galileo's time, most people believed that Earth was the center of the universe, and the sun and planets orbited around it.

In 1632, Galileo wrote a book supporting Copernicus's theory. The book was widely praised, but Galileo's ideas went against church teachings. Around 1633, a court in Rome made Galileo deny his beliefs. He was ordered to stay in his house the rest of his life. Some sources say that when Galileo was leaving the court, he said softly, "And yet it moves!" because he still believed in his theory.

Sources:

Couper, Heather; Henbest, Nigel. Space Encyclopedia. New York: DK Publishing, 1999.

Reid, Struan; Fara, Patricia. The Usborne Book of Scientists. Tulsa: EDC Publishing, 1997.

Clearly presents topic and introduces the main idea

Gives details that help explain the topic

Lists sources

Draft Use the model, your research notes, and your outline to write your report.

 Edit Work in pairs. Trade papers and read each other's reports. Use the editing checklist to evaluate each other's work.

EDITING CHECKLIST

Did you . . .

▶ state the main idea of your paper in the opening paragraph?

▶ include details to support the main idea in each paragraph?

▶ use passive verb forms correctly?

▶ use comparative and superlative adjectives correctly?

▶ present information in your own words?

▶ use quotations correctly?

▶ include a list of your sources?

 Revise Revise your report. Add information and correct mistakes if necessary.

 Publish Share your work with your teacher and classmates.

PROJECTS

Work in pairs or small groups. Choose one of these projects.

1. Paint a picture of a starry night. Use your own city or town as the background. When you have finished, share your work with the class.

2. Write a skit about one of the sun myths or another myth about a natural phenomenon. Practice the skit with classmates and perform it for your class.

3. Use the instructions in this unit to make a solar eclipse-viewing box. Show it to a family member and explain why it is necessary. Show how it works.

4. Create a "Reach for the Stars Hall of Fame." Use information from your research report to create a profile of an astronaut or astronomer. Download or copy a picture of the person or draw one. Display your picture and profile on a class bulletin board.

5. Create a star guide. Use the Internet and reference books to find out what constellations you can see from your town. Draw a map of the constellations and show where they would be located in the sky. On a clear night, go outside with a family member and see which constellations you can find. Report your experience to the class.

6. Visit a planetarium. Tell the class about your experience.

Adler Planetarium and
Astronomy Museum ▶

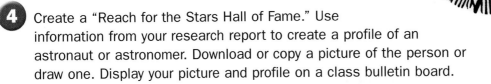

Further Reading

To find out more about the theme of this unit, choose from these reading suggestions.

Sally Ride: A Space Biography, **Barbara Kramer** Sally Ride became the first American woman to travel in space. This biography traces her life from childhood to the present. It focuses on her astronaut training and includes photographs of space flight.

Space Station: Accident on Mir, **Angela Royston** This is a true account of an accident on the Russian space station Mir in 1997. The book explains what led up to the event and describes how the crew worked together to avoid disaster. It also includes the experiences of American astronaut Mike Foale, who was onboard at the time.

Moon Landing: The Race for the Moon, **Carole Stott** This book gives us the history of space flight. It describes the time when the Americans were in competition with the Russians to put the first person on the moon. After covering the 1969 moon landing in full, the book brings us up-to-date with a discussion of current missions.

Stars, **Seymour Simon** In photo-essay format, *Stars* takes readers on a tour of the galaxies. The book describes ordinary stars such as our sun, as well as stars called red giants and white dwarfs. It also explains how stars form, go through various stages of growth, and die.

Star Wars: The Power of Myth, **David John (editor)** Throughout history people have told myths to explain the mysteries of the universe. In this book we learn about many myths that inspired the stories in the *Star Wars* series.

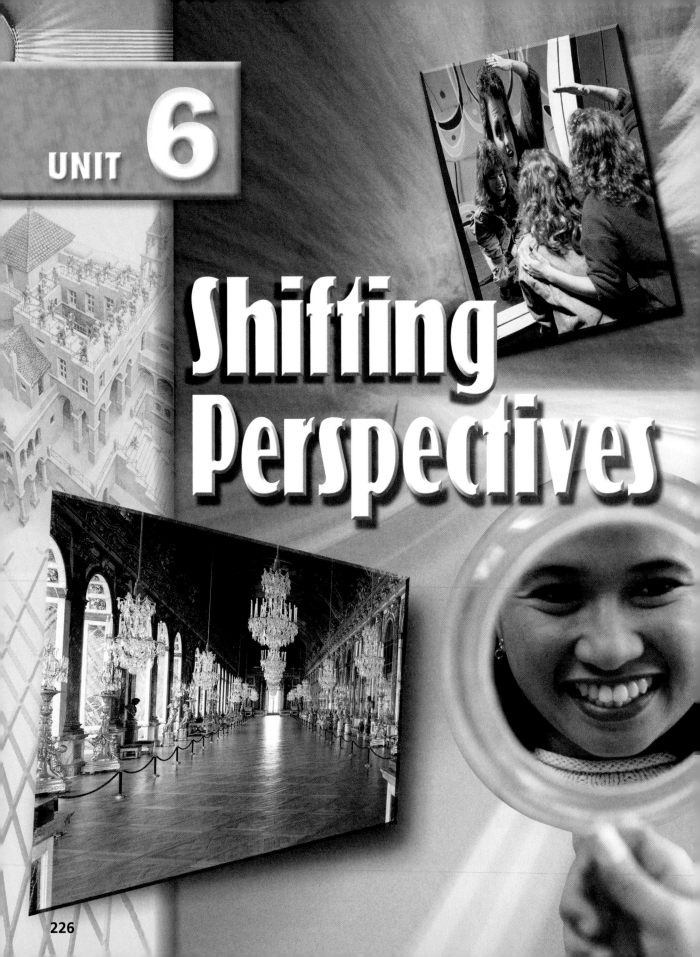

Shifting Perspectives

PART 1

■ "Light"

■ "A Reflection in Art: Jan van Eyck's Double Portrait"

■ "Mirror, Mirror: Mambo No. 5," Gustavo Pérez Firmat

PART 2

■ From *The Story of My Life*, Helen Keller

■ "Sowing the Seeds of Peace," Mandy Terc

Your perspective—or your view of something—often depends on where you are. If your position changes, so does your perspective. Think of how your perspective of the world now is different from what it was when you were a young child. Your perspective can also shift if you change your focus. Look at an ordinary leaf with a magnifying glass, and you will see details of the leaf's structure that you would not otherwise have seen.

In Part 1, you will read a science article about light rays—something that lets us see things. The article describes the nature of light and explains how different images are created and reflected. Then you will view a painting that shows a scene from two different perspectives. The third selection you will read tells of a restaurant in Miami, Florida, that is filled with mirrors from top to bottom.

In Part 2, you will read excerpts from Helen Keller's autobiography. Keller's life changed dramatically when she became ill as an infant and lost her ability to see and hear. This change in her life left Keller feeling angry and hopeless. Her perspective, however, shifted when she learned a way to communicate with others. Finally, you will read an article about a summer camp where girls from different countries—who have very different perspectives—come together to talk, to play, and to learn from one another.

Prepare to Read

OBJECTIVES

LANGUAGE DEVELOPMENT

Reading:
- Vocabulary building: *Context, dictionary skills*
- Reading strategy: *Monitoring comprehension*
- Text types: *Informational articles, essay*
- Compare and contrast

Writing:
- General and specific information
- Response to fine art

Listening/Speaking:
- Compare and contrast
- Share information about communities

Grammar:
- Subject/object pronouns

Viewing/Representing:
- Examine and interpret fine art

ACADEMIC CONTENT
- Science and art vocabulary
- Electromagnetic waves
- Jan van Eyck

BACKGROUND

"Light" is an informational science article. It gives facts about light and the way that light is reflected.

Have you ever seen waves moving across the ocean? Different kinds of energy can move through air, water, and even solid materials in the form of waves. In this section, you will read about electromagnetic waves. These are the waves that make up the light we see.

Make connections The chart lists different types of electromagnetic waves and gives facts about each. Look at the chart. Then answer the questions.

Type of Wave	Facts
Radio waves	• carry information through radio and television
Infrared waves	• heat from sun and fire • used in heat lamps and TV remote control
Ultraviolet waves	• too short for humans to see • cause sunburn and skin cancer
X rays	• can pass through the body • used to photograph bones
Gamma rays	• kill some cancer cells • contain much energy; produced by nuclear explosions

1. What types of waves would you find in your house?
2. What kinds of waves do doctors use?
3. What types of waves could be dangerous for people?
4. What waves would you feel if you were sitting near a fire?

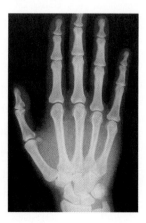

Color-enhanced X ray of hand ▶

LEARN KEY WORDS

absorbed
double
range
reflected
surface
transmitted

VOCABULARY

Read these sentences. Use the context to figure out the meaning of the **red** words. Use a dictionary to check your answers. Write each word and its meaning in your notebook.

1. The towel **absorbed** the spilled water, and now the table is dry.
2. You can see two movies for the price of one at a **double** feature.
3. That store has a wide **range** of CDs from many different countries.
4. When you stand by the lake, you can see the mountains **reflected** in the water.
5. The boat sailed across the **surface** of the lake.
6. Television shows are **transmitted** from the station to many peoples' homes.

READING STRATEGY

Monitoring Comprehension

Monitor, or check, **your comprehension** as you read. For example, ask yourself, "Did I understand that paragraph? What don't I understand?" If you find text that you don't understand, follow these steps:

- Reread the text.
- Try to paraphrase the text—put the information in your own words.
- Make a list of words or ideas that are hard to understand. Try to figure out their meanings from context; if you can't, look up the words in a dictionary.
- Write questions about things that you don't understand.
- Look for answers to your questions in the text or ask your teacher.

Science and Art

Preview the article and set your purpose for reading it. As you read, ask yourself questions to check your understanding. If you don't understand something, reread it and try to paraphrase it. Write questions about ideas you don't understand and make a list of words you don't know. Look for answers and definitions in the text.

Light

▲ When white light passes through a prism, it separates into colors.

How Does Light Travel?

Light travels from the sun to Earth in waves. These waves, called **electromagnetic waves**, are a form of energy that can travel through space. We talk about electromagnetic waves in terms of the length of the wave, or **wavelength**.

The **electromagnetic spectrum** is the name for the whole range of electromagnetic waves. It is organized by wavelength, from the longest electromagnetic waves to the shortest. The longest waves in the spectrum are radio waves. Then come infrared rays, visible light, ultraviolet rays, X rays, and gamma rays.

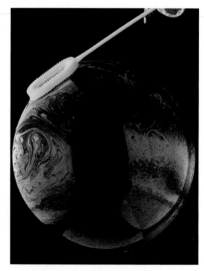

▲ Colors in a soap bubble

| Long ←— | **Wavelength** | —→ Short |

Radio waves | Infared rays | Ultraviolet rays | X rays | Gamma rays

Visible light

Red   Orange   Yellow   Green   Blue   Violet

▲ Figure 1. The electromagnetic spectrum

Visible light is the part of the electromagnetic spectrum that people can see. Visible light is only a small part of the electromagnetic spectrum. It is located between infrared rays and ultraviolet rays. Visible light is a mixture of all the colors we can see in a rainbow: red, orange, yellow, green, blue, and violet. When our eyes take in different wavelengths of light, they see different colors. Our eyes see the longest wavelengths of visible light as red. The shortest wavelengths are seen as violet.

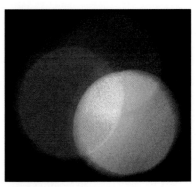

▲ Colors in visible light

What Happens When Light Strikes Objects?

When light **strikes** an object, the light can be reflected, or bounced off the object. The light might also be absorbed, or taken in by the object. Or the light can be transmitted, or passed through the object.

Objects that you cannot see through, such as wood and metal, are called **opaque**. When light strikes an opaque object, the light is either reflected or absorbed. You cannot see through an opaque object because light cannot pass through it. A glass object is **transparent**. When light strikes it, the light is allowed to pass through. As a result, you can see through the glass object.

---

strikes, hits

BEFORE YOU GO ON . . .

1 What electromagnetic waves have the longest wavelength? The shortest wavelength?

2 Compare and contrast an opaque object and a transparent object.

HOW ABOUT YOU?
• What are some transparent objects that you use every day?

▲ Spools of thread

▲ Glass and bottle containing milk

▲ Frog behind leaf

Other objects are **translucent**. When light strikes them, only some light passes through. When you look through a translucent object, you can see something behind it, but you cannot see the details clearly. Look at the pictures above. Which objects are opaque? Which are transparent? Which is translucent?

What Is Reflection?

All objects reflect light. This means that light bounces off of them. However, different objects reflect light in different ways.

Some objects allow you to see a reflection—or image—of something. For example, when you look at a mirror or a pool of water, you can see a reflection of yourself.

Other objects do not do this. For example, when you look at a wool sweater or a painted wall, you see only the object itself. What you see when you look at an object depends on how its surface reflects light.

To show how light travels and reflects, we can use straight lines to **represent** light rays. When **parallel** rays of light hit a smooth, or even, surface, all the rays are reflected at the same angle. This is called **regular reflection**. For example, when you look at a mirror, you see your own reflection. The light rays from your body hit the smooth surface of the mirror and are reflected regularly.

▲ Your image in a mirror is caused by rays of light that reflect regularly from the silver coating.

represent, stand for
parallel, two lines that stay the same distance apart and never touch

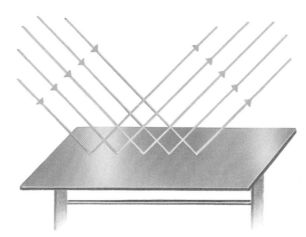

▲ Figure 2. When parallel rays of light strike a smooth surface, the reflection is regular.

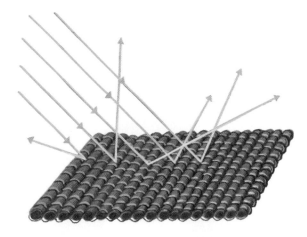

▲ Figure 3. When parallel rays of light strike an uneven surface, the reflection is diffuse.

When parallel rays of light hit a bumpy, or uneven, surface, each ray is reflected at a different angle. This is called **diffuse reflection**. Most objects reflect light diffusely because their surfaces are not completely smooth. For example, a wall may look smooth. But if you look carefully, you will see that its surface has many small bumps. These bumps cause the light to scatter, or to be reflected at different angles.

How Do Mirrors Work?

A mirror is a **sheet** of glass that has a smooth, silver-colored coating on one side. Glass is transparent, so light passes through it. However, the silver coating behind the glass is opaque. When light rays pass through the glass, they hit the smooth surface of the silver coating and all the rays are reflected regularly. The result is that you see an **image** in the mirror. An image is a copy of an object and is formed by reflected rays of light.

Mirrors can have a flat or curved shape. The shape of a mirror determines how the image will look. An image in a mirror can be the same size as the object, or it can be larger or smaller—depending on the mirror's shape.

---

sheet, thin piece

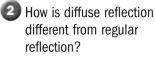

BEFORE YOU GO ON . . .

1 What happens when light strikes the surface of a translucent object?

2 How is diffuse reflection different from regular reflection?

HOW ABOUT YOU?

• Have you ever seen your reflection in objects other than a mirror? If so, describe the objects.

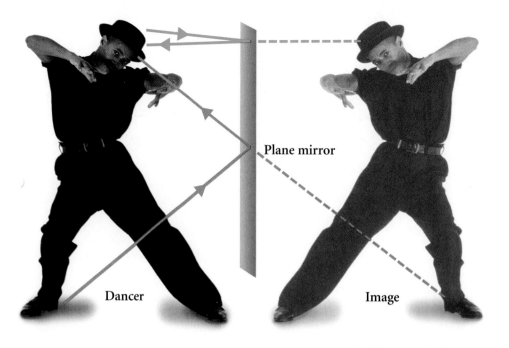

Plane mirror

Dancer

Image

▲ Figure 4. A plane mirror forms a virtual image.

A **plane mirror** has a flat surface. When you look into a plane mirror, you see an image that is the same size as you are. Your image **appears** to be the same distance behind the mirror as you are in front of it. The image you see in a plane mirror is called a **virtual image**. Virtual images are right side up, or upright. *Virtual* means something you can see, but does not really exist. You can't reach behind a mirror and touch your image.

Figure 4 shows how a plane mirror forms a virtual image of a dancer. Light rays reflected from the dancer strike the mirror. (The green and orange arrows show light rays from the top and bottom of the dancer.) The mirror reflects the rays toward the dancer's eyes. The brain **assumes** that the reflected rays have reached the eyes in a straight line.

The rays are reflected, but the brain interprets the rays as if they had come from behind the mirror. The dashed lines show the points from which the rays appear to come. Since the dashed lines appear to come from behind the mirror, this is where the dancer's image appears to be located.

---

appears, looks like
assumes, thinks that something is true; imagines

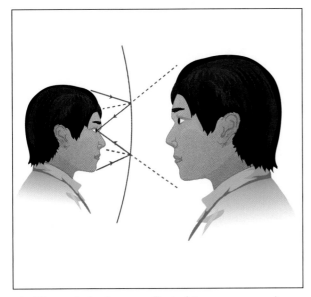

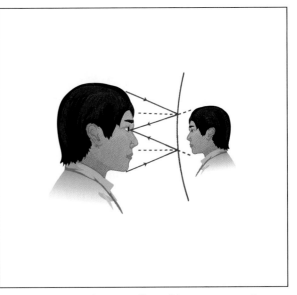

▲ **Figure 5.** An image reflected in a concave mirror   ▲ **Figure 6.** An image reflected in a convex mirror

Curved mirrors behave as though they were many, many little flat mirrors placed side by side, each at a slight angle to the one next to it. Unlike plane mirrors, curved mirrors create reflected images that are not the same size as the object being reflected. The images also appear farther away from or closer to the mirror than the object really is.

A **concave** mirror has a surface that curves inward. When you look into a concave mirror, the image you see of yourself appears larger than you really are. It also appears farther away from the mirror than you are actually standing. (See Figure 5.)

A **convex** mirror has a surface that curves outward. When you look into a convex mirror, the image you see is smaller than you are. And it appears closer to the mirror than you really are. (See Figure 6.)

Concave and convex mirrors are both useful in their own ways. Because concave mirrors enlarge the image, people use them when they are putting on makeup or shaving. Concave mirrors are also used as reflectors in flashlights and headlights. Convex mirrors let you see a large distance and a wide field of view, so they are used as rearview mirrors in cars and buses. They are also used as security mirrors in stores.

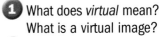

BEFORE YOU GO ON . . .

1 What does *virtual* mean? What is a virtual image?

2 Describe the image created by a concave mirror.

HOW ABOUT YOU?

● What are some different ways that you can use a mirror?

235

This article gives information about a famous painter and one of his paintings.

A REFLECTION IN ART:
Jan van Eyck's Double Portrait

Flemish artist Jan van Eyck (c. 1390–1441) painted the double portrait *Giovanni Arnolfini and His Bride,* shown on page 237. A **portrait** is a painting of one or more people. In 1434, Giovanni Arnolfini, a **wealthy** Italian banker, married Giovanna Cenami. Art historians believe that van Eyck painted this portrait as a celebration and **record** of their wedding.

Why is this painting called a *double* portrait? Look at the mirror on the wall behind the bride and groom. The mirror shows a reflection of the backs of Arnolfini and his bride. Now look closer. In the reflection, in front of the bride and groom, are two other people. They are probably **witnesses** to the wedding. So, there are two portraits: one outside the mirror, and one inside it!

---

wealthy, rich
record, something written down so you can look at it later
witnesses, people who see something happen

BEFORE YOU GO ON . . .

1 What is a portrait?

2 How does this painting make use of the concept of reflection?

HOW ABOUT YOU?

● Do you think the mirror in van Eyck's painting is a plane, concave, or convex mirror? Why?

Detail from *Giovanni Arnolfini and His Bride* ▶

Review and Practice

Reread "Light." Then read the statements below. Use the chart to compare and contrast the three types of mirrors. Copy the chart into your notebook. Complete the chart by writing the statements in the correct columns.

It has a surface that curves outward.
The image appears larger than the object is.
It has a surface that curves inward.
The image appears to be the same size as the object.
~~It has a flat surface.~~
The image appears smaller than the object is.

Plane Mirror	Concave Mirror	Convex Mirror
It has a flat surface.		

EXTENSION

Copy the chart into your notebook. Work with a partner. Look at the pictures at the top of page 232 and review the definitions of the words in the chart. List as many things as you can think of that fit in each category. Share your chart with another pair of students.

Opaque Objects	Transparent Objects	Translucent Objects

DISCUSSION

Discuss in pairs or small groups.

1. Imagine you are looking at an object. You can see some of the light shining through the object, but you cannot see things on the other side of the object. Is the object opaque, translucent, or transparent?

2. You see a reflection in a mirror. The reflection is smaller than the object being reflected. Are you seeing a reflection in a plane mirror, a convex mirror, or a concave mirror? How do you know?

3. Can mirrors create reflections that are not the way the object appears in real life? Explain.

In this section, you will read an essay. An essay is a short, nonfiction work in which a writer gives his or her ideas about a particular subject. In this essay, the writer tells about a restaurant in Miami. Read to find out how he feels about the restaurant and why he feels that way.

Mirror, Mirror: Mambo No. 5

Gustavo Pérez Firmat

One of the **landmarks** of Cuban Miami is a restaurant called Versailles, which has been located on Eighth Street and Thirty-fifth Avenue for many years. About the only thing this Versailles shares with its French **namesake** is that it has lots of mirrors on its walls. One goes to the Versailles not only to be seen, but to be multiplied. This **quaint**, **kitschy**, noisy restaurant that serves basic Cuban food is a paradise for the **self-absorbed**: the **Nirvana** of Little Havana. Because of the bright lights, even the windows reflect. The Versailles is a Cuban **panopticon**: you can lunch, but you can't hide. Who goes there wants to make a spectacle of himself (or herself). All the *ajiaco* you can eat and all the jewelry you can wear multiplied by the number of reflecting planes—and to top it off, a waitress who calls you *mi vida*.

▲ Hall of Mirrors in the French palace of Versailles

View of a restaurant from its mirrored ceiling ▼

landmarks, familiar sights
namesake, one having the same name as another
quaint, old-fashioned
kitschy, cheap or tacky
self-absorbed, people who like themselves very much
Nirvana, paradise
panopticon, a place where everyone can be observed
ajiaco, a spice used in Cuban cooking
mi vida, my life (term of endearment in Spanish)

Across the street at La Carreta, another popular restaurant, the food is the same (both establishments are owned by the same man) but the feel is different. Instead of mirrors La Carreta has booths. There you can **ensconce yourself** in a booth and not be faced with multiple images of yourself. But at the Versailles there is no choice but to **bask in self-reflective glory**.

For years I have **harbored the fantasy** that those mirrors **retain** the blurred image of everyone who has paraded before them. I think the mirrors have a memory, as when one turns off the TV and the shadowy figures remain on the screen. Every Cuban who has lived or set foot in Miami over the last three decades has, at one time or another, seen himself or herself reflected on those shiny surfaces. It's no coincidence that the Versailles sits only two blocks away from the Woodlawn Cemetery, which contains the remains of many Cuban notables, including Desi Arnaz's father, whose remains occupy a niche right above Gerardo Machado's. Has anybody ever counted the number of Cubans who have died in Miami? Miami is a Cuban city not only because of the number of Cubans who live there but also because of the number who have died there.

---

ensconce yourself, install yourself
bask in self-reflective glory, enjoy
   your own reflection
harbored the fantasy,
   had the idea
retain, keep

▲ Gerardo Machado (1871–1939) was president of Cuba from 1925 to 1933.

BEFORE YOU GO ON . . .

1 Why is the restaurant named after the Versailles palace in France?

2 Name the two famous Cubans the author mentions. Why was each famous?

HOW ABOUT YOU?

• Does the idea of dining in a restaurant filled with mirrors appeal to you? Why or why not?

◀ Desi Arnaz was a Cuban bandleader who was married to actress Lucille Ball. They starred in *I Love Lucy*, a popular television show of the 1950s and 1960s.

The Versailles is a **glistening mausoleum**. The history of Little Havana—**tragic**, **comic**, tragicomic—is written on those spectacular walls. This may have been why, when the mirrors came down in 1991, there was such an **uproar** that some of them had to be put back. The Hall of Mirrors is also a house of spirits. When the time comes for me to pay for my last *ajiaco,* I **intend** to disappear into one of the mirrors (I would prefer the one on the right, just above the espresso machine). My idea of **immortality** is to become a mirror image at the Versailles.

---

glistening, shiny
mausoleum, a place where dead people are buried
tragic, very sad
comic, funny
uproar, a lot of noise or angry protest against something
intend, plan
immortality, living forever

▲ Men playing chess in Maximo Gomez Park in Little Havana, Miami

BEFORE YOU GO ON . . .

1 What happened when the mirrors came off the walls of the restaurant in 1991?

2 What does the author say is his idea of immortality?

HOW ABOUT YOU?

● What other places do you know of that have the history of a city "written on" their walls?

Link the Readings

In Part 1, the readings and painting were about points of view, or different ways of seeing things. Copy the chart into your notebook and complete it.

Title of Selection	Genre	Fiction or Nonfiction	Purpose of Selection	Perspective
"Light"				
"A Reflection in Art: Jan van Eyck's Double Portrait"	*an article*			
"Mirror, Mirror: Mambo No. 5"				*Author believes that mirrors have a memory.*

DISCUSSION

Discuss in pairs or small groups.

1. All three texts discuss mirrors. Compare and contrast how the information is the same and how it is different.

2. What type of mirror—convex, concave, or plane—does the Versailles restaurant have on its walls? Why do you think so?

3. The Versailles restaurant is a special place to many people living in Little Havana in Miami. What place in your community is important to many people? Why?

Connect to Writing

GRAMMAR

Subject and Object Pronouns

Pronouns replace nouns. The form of the pronoun is different for **subject pronouns** and for **object pronouns**.

	Subject Pronouns	Object Pronouns
Singular	I, you, he, she, it	me, you, him, her, it
Plural	we, you, they	us, you, them

A subject pronoun replaces a noun that is the subject of a sentence.

subject nouns	subject pronouns
Jan van Eyck was a Flemish artist.	**He** painted portraits.
Versailles was the largest palace.	**It** was the center of the French government.
Some objects are transparent.	**They** allow the light to pass through.

An object pronoun replaces a noun that is an object (after the verb).

object nouns	object pronouns
I knew **Linda** liked Cuban food.	I took **her** to the Versailles restaurant.
We can see through **glass**.	Light passes through **it**.
You can see most **objects**.	Light bounces off **them**.

Practice

Copy the questions and answers into your notebook. Complete the answers with the correct pronouns.

1. Are violet and red two colors of visible light?

   Yes, _____ are. You can see _____ in a rainbow.

2. Is Maria in your class?

   Yes, _____ is. I sit next to _____.

3. Do you and José like the Versailles restaurant?

   Yes, _____ do. _____ has great food. Would you like to go there with _____?

4. When did Jan van Eyck paint *Giovanni Arnolfini and His Bride*?

   _____ painted _____ in 1434.

SKILLS FOR WRITING

Writing Responses

A response states your personal reaction to something, such as a text or a painting. It includes your thoughts and feelings about the work. One way to write a response to a painting is to begin with general information—information about the larger parts of the painting. Then you can give more specific information—details about smaller parts of the painting.

Read the paragraph below. Then discuss the questions.

Lauren Younkins

Giovanni Arnolfini and His Bride

Giovanni Arnolfini and His Bride, by Jan van Eyck, is an interesting painting. I like it because it's really two paintings in one. When you first look at it, you see a portrait of a man and a woman holding hands. They are dressed in old-fashioned clothes from around the fifteenth century. When you look at the painting more closely, you can see a mirror between Giovanni and his wife. In the mirror, you see both of them again, but this time, you see their backs. And you can see something that you couldn't see without looking in the mirror—you see two people who are witnessing their wedding. Van Eyck's painting can be seen from two perspectives—one from outside the mirror and another from inside it.

1. Which sentence tells the main idea of the paragraph?
2. Which sentences give general information about the whole painting?
3. Which sentences give specific information about smaller details?

WRITING ASSIGNMENT

Response

You will write a one-paragraph response to a painting.

1. **Read** Reread the student paragraph about *Giovanni Arnolfini and His Bride*. Use the Internet or the library to find a painting by one of these artists: Mary Cassatt, Diego Rivera, Remedios Varo, René Magritte, Georgia O'Keeffe, M. C. Escher, Edward Hopper, or Jacob Lawrence. Look at the painting carefully. What are your thoughts and feelings about it? Think about your main idea, and write a topic sentence.

Writing Strategy: Organizational Chart

A chart can help you organize general and specific information. Look at the chart the writer used to write a response to van Eyck's painting. Note that the writer underlined the title of the painting. When you write about a work of art, underline or italicize the title.

Main Idea: Jan van Eyck's painting is two paintings in one.
General Information (the larger picture):   • At first, you see a large portrait.   • Giovanni and his wife are holding hands.   • They are wearing old-fashioned clothes.
Specific Information (the smaller details):   • Look closely and you see the small portrait inside the mirror.   • The backs of Giovanni and his wife are reflected in the mirror.   • In the reflection, two witnesses are standing in front of the couple.

---

2. **Make a chart** In your notebook, write your main idea about the painting. Next, list your general ideas and feelings about it. Then list specific details about the painting that you like or find interesting.

3. **Write** Use your chart to write your response.

EDITING CHECKLIST

Did you . . .

▶ underline or italicize the painting's title?

▶ include a topic sentence?

▶ write first general and then specific information?

Check Your Knowledge

Language Development

1. What are some ways you can monitor your comprehension while reading?

2. Compare the two informational articles you read in Part 1. What kind of articles are they? What are they about? Which was more interesting to you? Why?

3. What is the difference between general and specific information? When you write, in what order do you organize general and specific information? Why?

4. Give an example of a sentence containing a subject pronoun, and of one containing an object pronoun.

5. What are some things you include when you write a response to fine art?

Academic Content

1. What new science and art vocabulary did you learn in Part 1? What do the words mean?

2. What are electromagnetic waves? Give examples of two kinds.

3. Is a glass window opaque, transparent, or translucent? What happens when light strikes a glass window?

4. What is a portrait? Who is Jan van Eyck?

◀ Hall of Mirrors at Versailles

247

PART 2 Prepare to Read

OBJECTIVES

LANGUAGE DEVELOPMENT

Reading:
- Vocabulary building: *Context, dictionary skills*
- Reading strategy: *Listening to texts*
- Text types: *Autobiography, social studies article*
- Literary element: *Point of view*

Writing:
- Plot chart
- Sentence variety
- Paragraph unity
- Personal narrative

Listening/Speaking:
- Listening to texts
- Summarize a story
- Cause and effect

Grammar:
- Compound and complex sentences

Viewing/Representing:
- Photographs

ACADEMIC CONTENT
- Social studies vocabulary
- Helen Keller
- Middle Eastern conflict

BACKGROUND

In this section, you will read excerpts from *The Story of My Life,* Helen Keller's autobiography. An autobiography is a story that a person writes about his or her own life.

When Helen Keller was nineteen months old, she became sick. Her sickness left her hearing impaired (unable to hear), sight impaired (unable to see), and speech impaired (unable to speak). When she was almost seven years old, a teacher came to live with her family. This teacher taught Helen how to communicate using the manual alphabet.

Make connections Look at the timeline. Then answer the questions.

1880: Born

1882: Loses sight and hearing

1887: Anne Sullivan teaches Helen to use language to communicate

1888: Goes with Anne Sullivan to the Perkins Institution for the Blind

1894: Attends a school for hearing-impaired people in New York

1904: Becomes the first hearing- and sight-impaired person to earn a college degree

1938: Publishes *Helen Keller's Journal,* a story she wrote about her life

1955: Publishes *Teacher,* a book about Anne Sullivan

1964: President Lyndon B. Johnson awards her the Presidential Medal of Freedom

1968: Dies

1. When was Helen Keller born? When did she die? How long did she live?
2. What book did Helen Keller publish in 1955? Who was the book about?
3. What special award did Helen Keller get in 1964?

248

LEARN KEY WORDS

barrier
defects
imitate
repentance
sorrow
tangible

VOCABULARY

Read these sentences. Use the context to figure out the meaning of the **red** words. Use a dictionary to check your answers. Write each word and its meaning in your notebook.

1. People talking loudly in the theater was a **barrier** to our enjoyment of the movie.
2. My report had no **defects**—it was perfect.
3. Some birds, such as parrots, **imitate** people and say words.
4. The child showed **repentance** when he said he was sorry for breaking the glass.
5. We all felt **sorrow** when our team lost the big game.
6. The clouds seemed so **tangible** that I felt I could touch them.

READING STRATEGY

Listening to Texts

When you listen to a text, it is important to use some of the same strategies that you use when you read a text. Try some of these steps as you listen.

- Listen to the story as it is read aloud. Don't read along in your book. Try to visualize as you listen. Don't worry about understanding every word. Think about the overall meaning of the story.

- Listen to the story a second time. This time, follow along in the text. Match the words you hear to the ones on the page.

- Reread the text on your own. Keep in mind your purpose for reading as you make sense of the text.

Autobiography

Listen to the story without following along in your book. Visualize. Try to get the main ideas of the story. Then listen a second time, following the text in your book. Then summarize the main events and ideas of the story in your own words.

from The Story of My Life

▲ This photograph was taken when Helen was seven years old.

Chapter 1

One **brief** spring, musical with the song of robin and mocking-bird, one summer rich in fruit and roses, one autumn of gold and crimson sped by and left their gifts at the feet of an eager, delighted child. Then, in the **dreary** month of February, came the illness which closed my eyes and ears and plunged me into the unconsciousness of a new-born baby. They called it acute congestion of the stomach and brain. The doctor thought I could not live. Early one morning, however, the fever left me as suddenly and mysteriously as it had come. There was great **rejoicing** in the family that morning, but no one, not even the doctor, knew that I should never see or hear again.

* * *

Gradually I got used to the silence and darkness that surrounded me and forgot that it had ever been different, until she became my teacher who was to set my spirit free. But during the first nineteen months of my life I had caught glimpses of broad, green fields, a **luminous** sky, trees and flowers which the darkness that followed could not wholly blot out. If we have once seen, "the day is ours, and what the day has shown."

---

brief, short
dreary, dull or boring
rejoicing, celebrating
luminous, glowing

Anne Sullivan was Helen Keller's teacher. They were friends until Sullivan died in 1936.

Chapter 3

My aunt made me a big doll out of towels. It was the most comical, shapeless thing, this **improvised** doll, with no nose, mouth, ears or eyes—nothing that even the imagination of a child could **convert** into a face. Curiously enough, the absence of eyes struck me more than all the other defects put together. I pointed this out to everybody with **provoking** persistency, but no one seemed equal to the task of providing the doll with eyes. A bright idea, however, shot into my mind, and the problem was solved. I tumbled off the seat and searched under it until I found my aunt's cape, which was trimmed with large beads. I pulled two beads off and indicated to her that I wanted her to sew them on my doll. She raised my hand to her eyes in a questioning way, and I nodded energetically. The beads were sewed in the right place and I could not contain myself for joy. . . .

✳ ✳ ✳

Chapter 4

The most important day I remember in all my life is the one on which my teacher, Anne Mansfield Sullivan, came to me. I am filled with wonder when I consider the **immeasurable** contrasts between the two lives which it connects. It was the third of March, 1887, three months before I was seven years old.

---

improvised, made without preparation, using what she had
convert, change
provoking, making someone angry or annoyed
immeasurable, enormous

LITERARY ELEMENT

Point of view refers to the narrator, or person telling the story. When a person tells a story using the pronoun *I*, the story is in the first-person point of view. Autobiographies use the first-person point of view. In other stories, the narrator uses pronouns such as *he* and *she* to refer to the characters. These stories are told from the third-person point of view.

BEFORE YOU GO ON . . .

1. What bothered Helen the most about her doll? How did she ask her aunt to fix the doll?

2. What does Helen say happened on the most important day in her life?

HOW ABOUT YOU?

- In what ways does Helen seem just like any other young girl?

251

On the afternoon of that eventful day, I stood on the porch, **dumb**, expectant. I guessed **vaguely** from my mother's signs and from the hurrying to and fro in the house that something unusual was about to happen, so I went to the door and waited on the steps. The afternoon sun penetrated the mass of honeysuckle that covered the porch, and fell on my upturned face. My fingers lingered almost unconsciously on the familiar leaves and blossoms which had just come forth to greet the sweet southern spring. I did not know what the future held of marvel or surprise for me. Anger and **bitterness** had preyed upon me continually for weeks and a deep **languor** had succeeded this **passionate** struggle.

Have you ever been at sea in a dense fog, when it seemed as if a tangible white darkness shut you in, and the great ship, tense and anxious, **groped** her way toward the shore with plummet and sounding-line, and you waited with beating heart for something to happen? I was like that ship before my education began, only I was without compass or sounding-line and had no way of knowing how near the harbor was. "Light! Give me light!" was the

▲ As an adult, Helen Keller traveled with Anne Sullivan to give lectures about her life.

---

dumb, unable to speak
vaguely, unclearly
bitterness, the feeling of being angry because of something that someone
    has done or said
languor, feeling of tiredness
passionate, having very
    strong feelings
groped, felt around for
    something

The Perkins Institution for the Blind teaches sight-impaired people ways to adapt to the world. ▶

wordless cry of my soul, and the light of love shone on me in that very hour.

I felt approaching footsteps, I stretched out my hand as I supposed to my mother. Someone took it, and I was caught up and held close in the arms of her who had come to reveal all things to me, and, more than all things else, to love me.

The morning after my teacher came she led me into her room and gave me a doll. The little blind children at the Perkins Institution had sent it and **Laura Bridgman** had dressed it, but I didn't know this until afterward. When I had played with it a little while, Miss Sullivan slowly spelled into my hand the word "d-o-l-l." I was at once interested in this finger play and tried to imitate it. When I finally succeeded in making the letters correctly I was flushed with childish pleasure and pride. Running downstairs to my mother I held up my hand and made the letters for doll. I did not know that I was spelling a word or even that words existed; I was simply making my fingers go in monkey-like imitation. In the days that followed I learned to spell in this **uncomprehending** way a great many words, among them, *pin, hat, cup* and a few verbs like *sit, stand* and *walk*. But my teacher had been with me several weeks before I understood that everything has a name.

One day, while I was playing with my new doll, Miss Sullivan put my big rag doll into my lap also, spelled "d-o-l-l" and tried to make me understand that "d-o-l-l" applied to both. Earlier in the day we had had a tussle over the words "m-u-g" and "w-a-t-e-r." Miss Sullivan had tried to impress it upon me that "m-u-g" is mug and that "w-a-t-e-r" is water, but I persisted in confounding the two. In **despair**, she had dropped the subject for the time, only to renew it at the first opportunity. I became **impatient** at her repeated attempts and, seizing the new

▲ The hands in this picture spell the word *doll.*

BEFORE YOU GO ON . . .

1 What did Helen compare herself to before Anne Sullivan came?

2 What were the first words that Helen learned to spell with her fingers? Why does she call this spelling "finger play"?

HOW ABOUT YOU?

● Have you ever felt like the ship Helen Keller describes on page 252? Explain.

Laura Bridgman, hearing- and sight-impaired woman who had learned to read and write at the Perkins Institution in the 1830s
uncomprehending, not understanding
despair, feeling very sad or having no hope
impatient, annoyed; irritated

▲ Keller, Sullivan, and Alexander Graham Bell in about 1894

▲ Keller, Sullivan, and Mark Twain in about 1902

▲ Keller holds her Oscar award for the documentary film *Helen Keller in Her Story*, about 1954.

doll, I dashed it upon the floor. I was keenly delighted when I felt the fragments of the broken doll at my feet. Neither sorrow nor regret followed my passionate outburst. I had not loved the doll. In the still, dark world in which I lived there was no strong **sentiment** or tenderness. I felt my teacher sweep the fragments to one side of the hearth, and I had a sense of satisfaction that the cause of my discomfort was removed. She brought me my hat, and I knew I was going out into the warm sunshine. This thought, if a wordless sensation may be called a thought, made me hop and skip with pleasure.

We walked down the path to the well-house, attracted by the fragrance of the honeysuckle with which it was covered. Someone was **drawing water** and my teacher placed my hand under the **spout**. As the cool stream gushed over one hand she spelled into the other the word *water*, first slowly, then rapidly. I stood still, my whole attention fixed upon the motions of her fingers. Suddenly I felt a misty consciousness as of something forgotten—a thrill of returning thought; and somehow the mystery of language was revealed to me. I knew then that "w-a-t-e-r"

▲ Anne Sullivan and Helen Keller visited the home of Alexander Graham Bell, the inventor of the telephone. Bell worked with hearing-impaired people.

---

sentiment, feeling or emotion
drawing water, getting water from a well
spout, part of a water pump where the water comes out

▲ A scene from *Helen Keller in Her Story,* showing Keller with dancer/choreographer Martha Graham and dancers

▲ President John F. Kennedy with Keller and her secretary, Evelyn Seide, in about 1961

meant the wonderful cool something that was flowing over my hand. That living word awakened my soul, gave it light, hope, joy, set it free! There were barriers still, it is true, but barriers that could in time be swept away.

I left the well-house eager to learn. Everything had a name, and each name gave birth to a new thought. As we returned to the house every object which I touched seemed to quiver with life. That was because I saw everything with strange, new sight that had come to me. On entering the door I remembered the doll I had broken. I felt my way to the hearth and picked up the pieces. I tried **vainly** to put them together. Then my eyes filled with tears; for I realized what I had done, and for the first time I felt repentance and sorrow.

I learned a great many new words that day. I do not remember what they all were; but I do know that *mother, father, sister,* and *teacher* were among them—words that were to make the world blossom for me, "like Aaron's rod, with flowers." It would have been difficult to find a happier child than I was as I lay in my crib at the close of that eventful day and lived over the joys it had brought me, and for the first time longed for a new day to come.

---

vainly, without success

BEFORE YOU GO ON . . .

1 What was the first word that Helen really understood?

2 How did learning one word change Helen's perspective?

HOW ABOUT YOU?

● Think about someone who taught you something new. What did the person do to teach you? How did learning it change you?

Review and Practice

The excerpts from *The Story of My Life* tell about a problem Helen Keller had and how she and others found a solution to the problem. Reread the text. Then copy the chart into your notebook. In the first box, describe Helen Keller's major problem in the story. You can use the text provided below as a model. In the second box, write about attempts to solve the problem. In the third box, tell how the problem was solved.

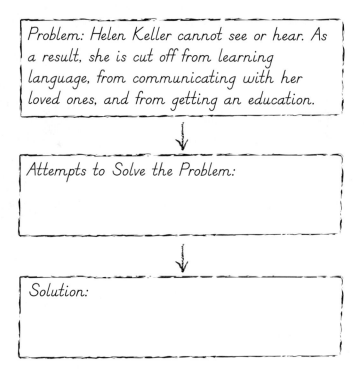

Problem: Helen Keller cannot see or hear. As a result, she is cut off from learning language, from communicating with her loved ones, and from getting an education.

Attempts to Solve the Problem:

Solution:

Use your completed chart to summarize the story with a partner.

EXTENSION

This story is written from Helen Keller's point of view. What would the story be like if Anne Sullivan told it instead of Helen Keller? Imagine that you are Anne Sullivan. Write a journal entry in your notebook. Write using Sullivan's point of view. Tell what happened when you were working with Helen Keller and how you felt about it. When you finish, read your journal entry to a partner.

DISCUSSION

Discuss in pairs or small groups.

1. What was Helen Keller's life like before she met Anne Sullivan? How did Sullivan change her life?

2. When Helen first broke her doll, she was pleased with herself. Later, however, she felt repentance. Why?

3. Why was it so important for Helen Keller to understand that the letters she was making with her fingers spelled words, and that the words were names for things?

◀ Helen Keller, age 12, with Anne Sullivan

This is a social studies informational text. It is a newsletter article about a special camp program. Look at the pictures to predict what the article is about. Then listen to the article.

Sowing the
Seeds of Peace

Mandy Terc

▲ Campers at Seeds of Peace International Camp

One rainy rest hour at a summer camp in Maine, fifteen-year-old Noor from the Palestinian West Bank was learning to write her name. She glanced back quickly at the example that sixteen-year-old Shirlee, a Jewish Israeli from a seaside town, had provided. After a few more seconds of intense writing, Noor triumphantly handed the piece of paper to me, her **bunk** counselor. Parading across the top of the paper in large, careful print were the Hebrew letters that spelled her Arabic name.

A spontaneous lesson on the Hebrew and Arabic alphabets probably does not happen at most summer camp bunks, but the Seeds of Peace International Camp challenges the traditional definition of what teenagers can learn and accomplish at a summer camp. Seeds of Peace brings Middle Eastern teenagers from Israel, the Palestinian National Authority, Jordan, Egypt, and other countries to Maine to help them **confront** the conflict and violence that has defined their region for more than fifty years.

At this camp, things like table and bunk assignments, sports teams and seating are never accidental. They are all part of encouraging **interaction**. Here, Israelis and Arabs

---

sowing, planting
bunk, cabin
confront, deal with in a direct way
interaction, action or communication between or among people

not only meet for the first time but also sleep side by side, share a sink and participate in group games. In the close quarters of tiny cabins and bunk beds, bunk counselors encourage the campers to ignore national and ethnic **boundaries** as they make friends with their immediate neighbors.

The three weeks spent in Maine combine ordinary camp activities with a daily two-hour coexistence session, during which trained **facilitators** encourage discussion of political and personal issues. The remainder of the day is spent in **traditional summer camp activities**.

Teenagers are asked to analyze questions that have **perplexed** world leaders, and even bedtime can become a political forum. In my bunk, I asked the girls to summarize one positive and one negative aspect of their day before going to sleep. Sometimes, the discussions were about quite ordinary and uncontroversial things.

At other times, our bedtime discussions reflected the complexity and difficulties of living with **perceived** enemies. On one occasion, Adar, a strongly nationalistic Israeli, began by expressing frustration with a Palestinian girl's comment that Israel unjustly occupied Jerusalem, which the Palestinian felt truly belonged to the Palestinian people.

Instantly, eight bodies snapped from snug sleeping positions to tense, upright postures. Jerusalem is the most **contentious** issue between the Arab and Israeli campers, and each girl in the bunk was poised to take this opportunity to talk about her opinion on the disputed city. Adar asked if all Palestinians refused to recognize Israelis as **legitimate** residents of the city.

Almost before Adar could finish her question, Aman was ready to answer. Aman is a strong, athletic Palestinian who does not waste her words. When she begins to speak,

▲ Campers relaxing in their bunk

---

boundaries, borders or barriers
facilitators, people who encourage discussion about specific topics
traditional summer camp activities, sports; games
perplexed, puzzled or confused
perceived, seeming to be a certain way
contentious, likely to cause argument and disagreement
legitimate, lawful or right

BEFORE YOU GO ON . . .

❶ How does the camp encourage campers to interact?

❷ What issue caused a serious discussion at bedtime?

HOW ABOUT YOU?

● Would you like to go to a summer camp? If so, what kind would you like to go to?

she is both **intimidating** and impressive as she defends her opinions.

Calm and **composed**, she explained to Adar that the presence of Muslim holy sites in Jerusalem meant that the Palestinians were the rightful **proprietors** of the city. With an equally rapid response, Adar reminded her that Jerusalem also contained Jewish holy sites.

Aman seemed prepared for this answer. "We would be very nice to you [the Jewish people]. We would always let you come visit your sites, just like all the other tourists," she replied.

Adar had no intention of allowing her people to become theoretical tourists in this debate: "Well, we have the city now," Adar said. "You can't just make us leave, because it's ours. We might decide to give some of it to the Palestinians, but it belongs to us now."

I spent such times in the bunk listening. I only **sporadically** interjected my voice, reminding them not to hold each other, as individuals, responsible for the actions of their governments.

The conversation eventually wound down. As the girls drifted off to sleep, I felt relieved. As much as I want the girls in my bunk to express all their concerns and thoughts, any conversation about such a sensitive issue keeps me tense. The bunk must feel safe but issues of conflict can't be ignored or downplayed. As a bunk counselor, I must provide campers with the safety and security they need to continue the process of breaking down barriers.

---

intimidating, threatening or scary
composed, thoughtful
proprietors, owners
sporadically, from time to time

About the Author

Mandy Terc

Mandy Terc has worked at the Seeds of Peace camp in Maine and also in Seeds of Peace's New York development office. She is currently a master's candidate at Harvard University's Center for Middle Eastern Studies.

BEFORE YOU GO ON . . .

1. What did the author do during the discussion?
2. How did the writer feel when the girls were finished with their discussion?

HOW ABOUT YOU?

- Do you like to discuss politics? Why or why not?

Link the Readings

REFLECTION

In Part 2, both texts you read talk about "breaking barriers." Think about the two readings as you copy the chart into your notebook and complete it.

Title of Selection	Genre	Fiction or Nonfiction	Purpose of Selection	What Are the "Barriers"?
From *The Story of My Life*				
"Sowing the Seeds of Peace"				

DISCUSSION

Discuss in pairs or small groups.

1. Helen Keller's outlook on life changed after she learned the word *water*. How did the learning of language lead to other positive changes in her life?

2. Describe a time when you met someone whose perspective was different from your own. What did you do to get along with that person? Did you try to understand that person's perspective?

3. Both of these texts are about learning to communicate with people. What does each text tell you about the importance of communicating with others?

Connect to Writing

GRAMMAR

Compound and Complex Sentences

Imagine that you read this article in your school newspaper.

Tigers Win

The Tigers won the basketball game. It was at the gym last night. It was really exciting. They beat the Lions. The Lions played well. The score was 66–64. Jason O'Neal made the winning basket for the Tigers. The Tigers play again next week. They play the Bulls. The Bulls have not lost a game this year.

The article gives information, but all the sentences are very similar. To make your writing more interesting, use a variety of sentence types.

1. Combine simple sentences to make **compound sentences**. Use *and* to give additional information. Use *but* to show contrasting information.

> The Tigers won the basketball game at the gym last night, **and** it was really exciting.
>
> The Lions played well, **but** Jason O'Neal made the winning basket for the Tigers.

2. Use relative pronouns *that, which,* and *who* to make **complex sentences**.

> The basketball game, **which** was at the gym last night, was really exciting.
>
> Jason O'Neal made the basket **that** won the game.
>
> Next week the Tigers play the Bulls, **who** have not lost a game this year.

Practice

Rewrite the article from the school newspaper in your notebook. Use the ideas for adding sentence variety. Add more details to the article. Then work with a partner and compare your articles.

SKILLS FOR WRITING

Focusing on Paragraph Unity

The topic sentence tells the main idea of a paragraph. It tells the reader what the paragraph is about. A paragraph has **unity** when all the other sentences support or develop the topic sentence. Paragraph unity is important because

- it helps the reader follow and understand the ideas, and
- it makes the paragraph easier to read.

Read the paragraph below. Then discuss the questions. As you read, be aware that there are some phrases or sentences that don't belong.

Natalia Dare

I used to be afraid to ride a horse. I remember when I overcame this, last summer, during July, at my summer camp. I also did many memorable things there. One day, the campers in my group, my counselor, and I went horseback riding. As usual, I sat and watched as the other campers rode around and enjoyed themselves. One of them was from Florida. Finally, after my counselor and riding teacher encouraged me many times, I decided to give it a try. At first I was hesitant, but then I found the courage and made a cautious attempt. To reassure me, my counselor rode behind my horse and the teacher rode in front, so I wasn't afraid. As the day came to an end, I realized that I could do anything if I tried.

Discuss these questions.
1. What is the main idea of the paragraph?
2. Which phrases or sentences don't belong in the paragraph? Why?

WRITING ASSIGNMENT

Personal Narrative

You will write a personal narrative about an experience that changed your perspective about something.

1. **Read** Think about Helen Keller's experiences and reread "Sowing the Seeds of Peace." What caused the people's perspectives to shift? Have you had an experience that made your perspective shift?

Writing Strategy: Plot Chart

A plot chart helps you organize the important events in a narrative before you write it. Look at the plot chart the student created for her paragraph about riding a horse at camp.

Setting:	at camp last summer
Characters:	myself, the other campers, our counselor, the riding teacher
Events:	I was afraid to ride a horse. I watched the other campers ride horses. My counselor and the riding teacher encouraged me to try to ride a horse. I finally tried to ride. My counselor rode behind my horse and the teacher rode in front of my horse, so I wasn't afraid.
Outcome:	I realized that I could do anything if I tried.

1. Where and when does the action take place?
2. Who are the characters?
3. What did the author learn from the events?

2. **Make a plot chart** Think about an experience that has shifted your perspective in some way. Make a plot chart to describe the setting, characters, events, and outcome.

3. **Write** Use your plot chart as your guide as you write your personal narrative.

EDITING CHECKLIST

Did you . . .

▶ include a main idea?
▶ include only sentences that support your main idea?
▶ use a variety of sentence structures and lengths?
▶ use first-person point of view?

Check Your Knowledge

Language Development

1. What are some similarities and differences between reading a text and listening to a text?

2. What is an autobiography? Why does an autobiography use first-person point of view?

3. Why is it important to use a variety of sentence types in your writing?

4. What is paragraph unity? Why is paragraph unity important?

5. How can a plot chart help you write a personal narrative?

Academic Content

1. What new social studies vocabulary did you learn in Part 2? What do the words mean?

2. What did Anne Sullivan do to help Helen Keller? Do you think that Helen could have learned language on her own? Why or why not?

3. Why do people go to Seeds of Peace International Camp? Do you think that the camp program can make a difference in the world? Why or why not?

▲ Girls having a conversation using American Sign Language

Put It All Together

GROUP PRESENTATION

You will make a group presentation about a person whose life and perspective changed because of an important event or experience.

 Think about it Think of a person whose perspective changed because of something important that happened to him or her. The person can be someone famous, a friend, or a family member.

Working in small groups, talk about the people you chose. Then choose one person for your presentation. Make a list of facts that you want to include.

2 **Organize** Decide how to organize your presentation. Think about these questions.

- What events in the person's life are you going to talk about?

- What visual aids will you use?

- In what order will you present the information?

3 **Practice** In your group, take turns practicing presenting. Ask other group members to listen and make suggestions.

4 **Present and evaluate** Make your presentation to the class. As each group finishes, evaluate the presentation. Did it give enough information about the person and his or her experiences?

SPEAKING TIPS

Begin by getting your audience's attention. Here are some ideas.
- Use a quote. For example: *"I'm the greatest!" shouted Mohammad Ali.*
- Make a surprising statement, such as: *Vincent van Gogh sold only one painting during his lifetime.*

LISTENING TIPS

- Take notes on new or interesting information.
- After the presentation, summarize the speakers' main ideas. Do you understand why the group chose the person and how the event changed him or her? If not, ask the group to clarify.

WRITING WORKSHOP

SHORT STORY

A short story is a short work of fiction. The writer usually presents a short plot, or sequence of events. In the plot, one or more characters usually experience a problem or conflict. A short story usually has a clear beginning, middle, and end. The writer's purpose is to entertain, to teach, or to show something about life.

A short story usually includes the following:

- characters
- a setting
- a series of events that includes a problem or conflict for one or more characters
- dialogue
- a beginning, a middle, and an end

You will write a short story in which something happens that changes a character's perspective. Read the model and follow the steps below.

 1 **Prewrite** Think about the people in the group presentations and about your own experience. What experiences might change the way a person looks at his or her life? Make a list of ideas.

Discuss ideas with a partner. Do you want to base your story on something that really happened to you or someone you know? Would you rather write about something from your imagination?

Choose a story idea. Then use a plot chart to plan the characters, setting, major events, and outcome of the story.

WRITING TIPS

Dialogue can make your story more interesting to read.
- Remember to put dialogue in quotation marks.
- Use different reporting verbs, such as *said, added, shouted, asked,* and *whispered,* to add detail and variety to your dialogue.
- Write dialogue that sounds natural, the way people really talk. Say your dialogue aloud to yourself to make sure that it is natural.

Before you write, read the model. Notice the characteristics of a short story:

Holly Sihombing

The View from the Front of the Classroom

It was her first day. Miss Taylor walked to the front of the second-grade classroom. She swallowed hard. Twenty pairs of eyes watched her.

"Hello, class," she squeaked. "I'm Miss Taylor, your art teacher for the next two weeks." She explained the project as the children talked. "Let's begin!" she said bravely. Suddenly, questions were flying.

"Miss Taylor! What am I supposed to do?"

"What are we making?"

"How do we do this?"

Children tugged at her. Miss Taylor rushed from child to child. When the bell rang, they ran out, leaving a mess behind them. Miss Taylor wondered how she would get through the next two weeks.

She got through those weeks and changed back to "Ashley," a seventh-grade student who had completed her school-service project. But she was not the same. Now she knew how hard her teachers worked. In her heart, Ashley thanked them for their dedication and for inspiring her to work hard, too.

main character

beginning

setting

middle

dialogue

problem or conflict

end

2 **Draft** Use the model and your plot chart to write your short story.

3 **Edit** Work with a partner. Trade papers and read each other's stories. Use the editing checklist to evaluate each other's work.

EDITING CHECKLIST
Did you . . .

▶ use a variety of sentence types?

▶ include sentences that are all related to the story?

▶ include realistic dialogue in quotation marks?

▶ use pronouns correctly?

▶ correct errors in spelling and punctuation?

4 **Revise** Revise your story. Add details or correct mistakes, if necessary.

5 **Publish** Share your work with your teacher and classmates.

PROJECTS

Work in pairs or small groups.
Choose one of these projects.

1 Read the rest of Helen Keller's autobiography, *The Story of My Life*. Tell the class more about Helen Keller's life. What else did she accomplish? How did Anne Sullivan stay involved in her life?

2 Start a classroom "library" with reports about books that tell about people whose outlook on life shifted dramatically. See the list of book titles on page 271 for some ideas.

3 Create a brochure for the Seeds of Peace International Camp. Your brochure should make people understand what makes this camp special.

4 Use the Internet to find out more about the study of light. For example, look for information about scientists who study light or about the uses of different types of light. Report your findings to the class.

5 The Versailles restaurant is an important place to many people who view life from the perspective of their Miami neighborhood. The restaurant is part of their culture. Is there a place in your city or town that is important to you or that reflects your culture? Write a description of the place. What would people find if they visited that place? Your description could be a page in a guide to your city.

6 Use the Internet and reference books to find out more about Jan van Eyck and his paintings. Share what you learn with the class in a brief oral report.

Further Reading

To find out more about the theme of this unit, choose from these reading suggestions.

***Zeely,* Virginia Hamilton** Geeder stays at her uncle's farm and becomes fascinated with a beautiful woman named Zeely. Geeder imagines that Zeely is a queen from Africa and that Geeder is her best friend. When Zeely finally talks about her life and her heritage, Geeder sees Zeely in a totally new light.

***Run Away Home,* Patricia C. McKissack** Sarah Crossman, an African-American girl, sees an Apache boy escape from a train taking him to a reservation. When her family adopts the boy, Sarah is not exactly thrilled to have a new brother. But Sarah grows to appreciate Sky as he helps her family fight a common enemy: racial discrimination.

***The Canterbury Tales,* Geoffrey Chaucer** The setting of this book is England in the fourteenth century. A group of people traveling together for five days tell stories to pass the time. Their stories show that the travelers have very different outlooks on life.

***Silas Marner,* George Eliot** Silas Marner is a lonely, bitter man with no friends. All he does is work, and all he cares about is money. Then his money is stolen. Soon after, he finds an abandoned baby. He adopts the baby and decides to raise her as his own daughter. From that point on, his perspective begins to change.

***The View from Saturday,* E. L. Konigsburg** This book is told from four different characters' perspectives. Each character tells his or her part of the story. These four characters are sure they have nothing in common—until they begin to see each other in a new way.

Glossary

ACTIVE VOICE /ak′tiv vois/
In the active voice, the subject of the sentence is the performer of the action: *Firefighters rescue people from burning buildings. (See also* Passive voice.)

ADJECTIVE /aj′ik tiv/
An adjective describes nouns (people, places, and things) or pronouns. In the sentence *I have a blue car,* the word *blue* is an adjective.

ADVERB /ad′vûrb/
An adverb describes a verb, an adjective, or another adverb. Adverbs answer the questions *where, when, in what way,* or *to what extent.*

ALLITERATION /ə lit′e rā′shən/
Alliteration is the repetition of initial consonant sounds. Writers use alliteration to draw attention to certain words or ideas, to imitate sounds, and to create musical effects.

ANALYZING TEXT STRUCTURE
/an′ə lī′ zing tekst struk′chər/
Analyzing the structure of a text can help you determine what kind of text you are reading. Poems, stories, and plays all look different.

ARTICLE /är′ti kəl/
An article is a piece of nonfiction writing in a newspaper, magazine, etc.

AUTOBIOGRAPHY /ȯ′tə bī og′rə fē/
An autobiography is the story of the writer's own life, told by the writer. Autobiographical writing may tell about the person's whole life or only a part of it. Because autobiographies are about real people and events, they are a form of nonfiction. Most autobiographies are written in the first person.

BASE FORM /bās fôrm/
The base form, or simple form, of a verb has no added ending (*-s, -ing, -ed*). *Talk* is the base form of the verb *talk.* (Other forms of *talk* are *talks, talking,* and *talked.*)

BIOGRAPHY /bī og′rə fē/
A biography is the nonfictional story of a person's life told by another person. Biographies are often about famous or admirable people.

CHARACTER /kar′ik tər/
A character is a person or an animal that takes part in the action of a literary work.

CHARACTERIZATION /kar′ik tər ə zā′shən/
Characterization is the act of creating or developing a character. Characterization can be direct or indirect. In the direct method, writers state the character's traits. In the indirect method, writers show what a character is like by describing what he or she says and does, or by what others say about him or her.

COMPARATIVE /kəm par′ə tiv/
A comparative is an adjective or adverb used to compare two things, as in the sentence *Julia is taller than Bob.* The word *taller* is the comparative form of the adjective *tall. (See also* Superlative.)

COMPARING AND CONTRASTING
/kəm pâr′ing and kən trast′ing/
Comparing and contrasting is one way an author conveys important ideas. For example, to show how a character has developed, an author might compare and contrast the character's new attitude toward something with a previous attitude that he or she has outgrown.

COMPLEX SENTENCE
/kom′pleks sen′təns/
A complex sentence is made up of an independent clause and one or more dependent clauses.

COMPOUND SENTENCE
/kom′pound sen′təns/
A compound sentence is made up of two or more independent clauses joined by a comma and a coordinating conjunction *(and, but, so, for,* and *or). (See also* Coordinating conjunction.)

CONFLICT /kon′flikt/
A conflict is a struggle between opposing forces. Conflict is the main problem in a story. It is also one of the most important story elements because it sets the story's plot in motion. Conflict can be between characters or between groups of people. It can also be a struggle between a character and a force of nature.

CONTRACTION /kən trak′shən/
A contraction is two words combined into one with an apostrophe. The apostrophe takes the place of the missing letter(s). For example, the contraction of *you are* is *you're.* Contractions are used in speaking and informal writing.

COORDINATING CONJUNCTION
/kō ôrd′nā′ting kən jungk′shən/
A coordinating conjunction joins two independent clauses in a compound sentence. The words *and, but, so,* and *or* are coordinating conjunctions.

DEPENDENT CLAUSE /di pen′dənt klȯz/
A dependent clause has a subject and a verb, but does not stand alone as a complete sentence. A dependent clause usually begins with a subordinating conjunction, such as *because, before, after, when, while, although,* and *if.*

DESCRIPTIVE ESSAY /di skrip′tiv es′ā/
In a descriptive essay, descriptive details and adjectives help the reader visualize what a person, place, or thing is like.

DIALOGUE /dī′ə lȯg/
A dialogue is a conversation between characters. In poems, novels, and short stories, dialogue is usually shown by quotation marks (" ") to indicate a speaker's exact words. In a play, dialogue follows the names of characters, and no quotation marks are used.

DIARY /dī′ə rē/
A diary is a type of book in which you write each day about your personal thoughts, things that happened to you, or things that you did.

ESSAY /es′ā/
An essay is a short nonfiction work in which a writer states his or her personal ideas about a particular subject.

EXCERPT /ek′sėrpt//
An excerpt is a short passage or section taken from a longer text, such as a letter, a book, an article, a poem, a play, a speech, etc.

FABLE /fā′bəl/
A fable is a brief story or poem, usually with animal characters, that teaches a moral, or lesson. The moral is usually stated at the end of the fable.

FICTION /fik′shən/
Fiction is prose writing that tells about imaginary characters and events. Short stories and novels are works of fiction.

FLASHBACK /flash′bak′/
A flashback is a scene within a story that interrupts the sequence of events, to tell about something that happened in the past.

GENRE /jän′rə/
A genre is a division or type of literature. Literature is commonly divided into three major genres: poetry, prose (fiction and nonfiction), and drama.

HERO /HEROINE /hir′ō /her′ō ən/
A hero or heroine is a character in a story whose actions are inspiring, or noble. A hero or heroine often struggles to solve or overcome a problem.

HISTORICAL FICTION
/hi stôr′ə kəl fik′shən/
In historical fiction, real events, places, or people are incorporated into a fictional or made-up story.

HYPERBOLE /hī pėr′bə lē/
Hyperbole is a way of describing something by exaggerating on purpose—saying that it is much bigger, smaller, faster, or in some other way more than it really is: *I'm so hungry, I could eat a horse.*

IDENTIFYING CAUSES AND EFFECTS
/ī den′tə fī ing kȯz′əz and ə fekts′/
Identifying causes and effects as you read can help you better understand a text. Most fiction and nonfiction texts tell about events that happen. Why an event happens is a cause. What happens as a result of a cause is an effect. The words *so* and *because* often signal causes and effects.

IMPERATIVE /im per′ə tiv/
An imperative is the form of a verb used for giving an instruction, a direction, or an order: *Give me the ball. Turn to the right. Come here!*

INDEPENDENT CLAUSE
/in′di pen′dənt klȯz/
An independent clause contains a subject and a verb and can stand alone as a sentence.

INFORMATIONAL TEXT
/in′fər mā′shən əl tekst/
An informational text is a nonfiction text. It is about real facts or events and its purpose is to inform the reader.

INTERVIEW /in′tər vyü/
An interview is a conversation in which a person learns information about someone. Usually, the person doing the interviewing asks questions and records the other person's answers.

LETTER /let′ər/
A letter is a written communication from one person to another. In personal letters, the writer shares information and his or her thoughts and feelings with one other person or group.

LISTENING TO TEXTS
/lis′ning tü teksts/
When you listen to a text being read aloud, concentrate on your listening skills. Close your eyes and try to visualize what you hear. Do not read along in your book until you have heard the entire selection once.

MAKING INFERENCES
/ma′king in′fər ən səz/
Making inferences, or inferring, is making logical guesses based on what the author tells you. Your own knowledge and experience will help you make inferences.

METAPHOR /met′ə fôr/
A metaphor is a figure of speech used to describe something as though it were something else. A metaphor compares two things without using the word *like* or *as*: *Love is a rose. Hope is a thing with feathers.* (*See also* Simile.)

MODAL /mō′dəl/
A modal is a type of helping verb. There are several modals, such as *can, should, could, would,* and *must.* Modals are placed before the main verb. *Should* is a modal of advice. It is used to talk about the correct or appropriate thing to do: *You should think before speaking.*

MONITORING COMPREHENSION
/mon′ə tə ring kom′ pri hen′shən/
Monitoring, or checking, your comprehension as you read can help you be a better reader. As you read, ask yourself questions to check your understanding. If you don't understand something, reread it and try to paraphrase it. Write questions about ideas you don't understand and look for answers in the text.

MOOD /müd/
Mood, or atmosphere, is the feeling created in the reader by a literary work or passage. The mood can be sad, funny, scary, tense, happy, hopeless, etc.

MYSTERY /mis′tər ē/
A mystery is something that is difficult to understand or explain. In a mystery story, the characters as well as the readers are given clues, or hints, to solve, or figure out, the mystery.

MYTH /mith/
A myth is a short fictional tale. Myths explain the actions of gods and heroes or the origins of elements of nature. Their purpose is to entertain and instruct. Every ancient culture has its collection of myths, or mythology, that is passed from parents to children as part of the oral tradition.

NARRATIVE /nar′ə tiv/
A narrative is a story that can be either fiction or nonfiction. Novels and short stories are fictional narratives. Biographies and autobiographies are nonfiction narratives. In a personal narrative, the writer tells about something he or she experienced.

NARRATOR /nar′ ā tər/
A narrator is a speaker or character who tells a story. The narrator sometimes takes part in the action while telling the story. Other times, the narrator is outside the action and just speaks about it.

NONFICTION /non fik′shən/
Nonfiction is prose writing that tells about real people, places, objects, or events. Biographies, reports, and newspaper articles are examples of nonfiction.

NOUN /noun/
A noun is the name of a person, thing, place, or animal. *Plane, building,* and *child* are common nouns. *Robert, Chicago,* and *Puerto Rico* are proper nouns.

NOVEL /nov′əl/
A novel is a long work of fiction. Novels contain such elements as characters, plot, conflict, and setting. The writer develops these elements in the novel.

OBJECT PRONOUN /ob′jikt prō′noun/
Object pronouns *(me, you, him, her, it, us, you, them)* are used as objects in sentences: *John took the ball and gave it to me.*

PASSIVE VOICE /pas′iv vois/
In the passive voice, the subject of the sentence receives the action: *The ball was caught by the outfielder.* (*See also* Active voice.)

PERSONIFICATION
/pər son′ə fə kā′shən/
Personification is giving human traits to animals or objects.

PLAY /plā/
A play is a story performed live by people in a theater.

PLAYWRIGHT /plā′rīt/
A playwright is a person who writes plays.

PLOT /plot/
A plot is a sequence of connected events in a fictional story. In most stories, the plot has characters and a main problem or conflict. After the problem is introduced, it grows until a turning point, or climax, when a character tries to solve the problem. The end of the story usually follows the climax.

POEM /pō′əm/
A poem is a piece of writing that uses a pattern of words and sounds to express ideas, experiences, and emotions. Poems are written in lines. Groups of these lines are called stanzas or verses. Poems make up the genre of literature called poetry.

POINT OF VIEW /point ov vyü/
A narrator tells a story from his or her point of view. In the first-person point of view, the narrator tells the story using *I* and *my*. In the third-person point of view, the narrator tells someone else's story using *he* or *she* and *his* or *her*.

POSSESSIVE ADJECTIVE
/pə zes′iv aj′ik tiv/
A possessive adjective is the possessive form of a personal pronoun *(my, your, his, her, its, our, your, their)*.

POSSESSIVE PRONOUN
/pə zes′iv prō′noun/
A possessive pronoun takes the place of a possessive adjective + a noun. *Mine, yours, his, hers, ours, yours,* and *theirs* are possessive pronouns.

PREPOSITION /prep′ə zish′ən/
A preposition is a short connecting word, such as *to, with, from, in,* and *for* that is always followed by a noun or pronoun: *Amy's mother drives her to school. Amy walks back from school with friends.*

PREPOSITIONAL PHRASE
/prep′ə zish′ə nəl frāz/
A prepositional phrase is a preposition + a noun or pronoun. Prepositional phrases are used to show location, time, or description: *My family lives in the city* (location); *The movie starts at noon* (time); *This is a book about animals* (description).

PRESENT PERFECT /prez′nt pėr′fikt/
A verb in the present perfect talks about an action that happened at an indefinite time in the past: *He has traveled around the world.* The present perfect can also describe an action that started in the past and continues into the present (used with *for* or *since*): *She has been married for many years. She has been married since 1958.*

PRESENT PROGRESSIVE
/prez′nt prə gres′iv/
A verb in the present progressive describes an action that is happening now: *I am eating my lunch. It is raining today.*

PREVIEWING /prē′ vyü ing/
Previewing a text helps you set your purpose for reading. To preview a text, read the title and subtitles. Look at the photos and illustrations and read the captions. Ask yourself: *What will this text be about? What do I already know about this topic?*

PRONOUN /prō′noun/
A pronoun is a word used instead of a noun, to avoid repeating the noun: *Carlos goes to school. He likes it. He* replaces the proper noun *Carlos; it* replaces the noun *school.*

PROSE /prōz/
Prose is the ordinary form of written language. Most writing that is not poetry, drama, or song is considered prose. Prose is one of the major genres of literature and occurs in two forms—fiction and nonfiction.

PUNCTUATION /pungk′chü ā′shen/
Punctuation is the set of signs or marks, such as periods and commas, used to divide writing into phrases and sentences so that the meaning is clear. Besides periods and commas, common punctuation marks include exclamation points, question marks, hyphens, semicolons, and colons.

QUOTATION /kwō tā′shen/
A quotation is a speaker's exact words repeated in a text. The exact words are written between quotation marks: *Bill said, "I won't be going to school tomorrow."*

REAL CONDITIONAL /rē′əl kən dish′ə nəl/
Real conditional sentences contain a main clause and an *if* clause. The *if* clause states a condition. The main clause states the result of that condition: *If we win this game (if* clause), *we will go to the championship* (main clause).

RHYME /rīm/
Rhyme is the repetition of sounds at the ends of words. Many poems contain end rhymes, or rhyming words at the ends of lines.

SENTENCE /sen′təns/
A sentence is a group of words with a subject and a verb. A sentence expresses a complete thought.

SEQUENCE WORDS /sē′kwəns wėrdz/
Sequence words help show the order of steps or events. Some common sequence words are *first, second, next, then, after that,* and *finally: First, you should finish your homework. After that, you can go meet your friends.*

SETTING /set′ing/
The setting of a literary work is the time and place of the action. The setting includes all the details of a place and time—the year, the time of day, even the weather. The place may be a specific country, state, region, community, neighborhood, building, institution, or home. In most stories, the setting serves as a context in which characters interact. Setting can also help create a feeling, mood, or atmosphere.

SHORT STORY /shôrt stôr′ē/
A short story is a brief work of fiction. Like a
novel, a short story presents a sequence of
events, or plot. The events in a short story
usually communicate a message about life
or human nature.

SIMILE /sim′ə lē/
A simile is a figure of speech that uses *like*
or *as* to compare two different things in an
unusual way: *Her hair was like spun gold.*

SIMPLE PAST /sim′pəl past/
Verbs in the simple past are used to tell
about an action that happened in the past
and is completed: *The boy ate the apple.
The girl walked up the hill.*

SKIMMING /skim′ing/
Skimming a text can help you find the main
ideas quickly. To skim, read quickly without
stopping at words you don't understand. In
each section or paragraph, look for the topic
sentence—the sentence that tells you the
main idea.

SONG /sȯng/
A song is a piece of music made especially
for singing.

STAGE DIRECTIONS /stāj də rek′shənz/
Stage directions are notes included in a
drama to describe how the work is to be
performed or staged. Stage directions are
usually printed in italics and enclosed within
parentheses or brackets. Some stage
directions describe the movements and
costumes, as well as the emotional states
and ways of speaking of the characters.

SUBJECT PRONOUN /sub′jikt prō′noun/
Subject pronouns can be singular or plural.
Singular pronouns (*I, you, he, she, it*) refer to
singular nouns: *Roberto walks to school
because it is only a block away.* Plural
pronouns *(we, you, they)* refer to plural
nouns: *Our parents went to the store. They
will be back soon.*

SUBJECT-VERB AGREEMENT
/sub′jikt vȯrb ə grē′mənt/
The rule in grammar for subject-verb
agreement states that the subject (or
subjects) and verb in a sentence must agree
in number: *A man runs. Two men run. A tall
man and a short woman run.*

SUMMARIZING /sum′ə rīz′ing/
Summarizing a text is restating the main
ideas in your own words. Summarizing can
be especially helpful if the text is difficult or
the ideas are new to you.

SUMMARY /sum′ə rē/
A summary is a brief statement that gives the
main points of an event or literary work.

SUPERLATIVE /sə pėr′lə tiv/
A superlative is an adjective used to
compare three or more things, as in the
sentence *Jake is the biggest dog in the
neighborhood.* The word *biggest* is the
superlative form of the word *big.*

SUSPENSE /sə spens′/
Suspense is a feeling of uncertainty about
the outcome of events in a literary work.
Stories with suspense make the readers ask,
"What will happen next?"

TAKING NOTES /tāk′ing nōts/
Taking notes as you read can help you focus your attention and remember facts more easily. When you take notes, don't write complete sentences and use abbreviations when possible.

TALL TALE /tȯl tāl/
Tall tales, like myths, are part of the oral tradition. They involve characters with highly exaggerated abilities and qualities. Pecos Bill, a cowboy raised by coyotes, and Paul Bunyan, a mighty lumberjack, are examples of characters from tall tales.

THEME /thēm/
The theme is the central idea, or message, of a work of literature. A theme can usually be expressed as a generalization, or general statement, about human beings or about life. The theme is not just a summary of the plot. It is the writer's main point.

TIME PHRASE /tīm frāz/
Time phrases tell the reader when an event happened: *Yesterday*, we went to see a movie. *Last night*, we watched television. *Next week*, we will go to see my grandmother.

USING KNOWLEDGE AND EXPERIENCE TO PREDICT
/yüz′ing nol′ij and ek spir′ēəns tü pri dikt′/
Using your own knowledge and experience can help you predict what is in a text. Predicting and then reading to confirm your predictions can help you become a more active and more effective reader.

USING A K-W-L-H CHART
/yüz′ing ə K-W-L-H chärt/
Using a K-W-L-H chart can help you read more actively. To complete a K-W-L-H chart, you need to do the following: list facts you know, ask questions to focus your reading, record facts you learn in the text, and think about how you learned these facts.

VERB /vėrb/
The verb is the word in a sentence that describes an action, a fact, or a state: *Tom is eating his lunch* (action). *New York has many tall buildings* (fact). *Mary feels sleepy* (state).

VISUALIZING /vizh′ü ə līz′ing/
Visualizing means picturing something in your mind. Good writers help readers visualize by choosing colorful words that create vivid pictures. Visualizing a story or other text can help you understand it better and enjoy it more.

Index

Acknowledgments

American Camping Association, Inc. "Understanding Cultural Differences" by Sandy Cameron, reprinted from *Camping Magazine* by permission of the American Camping Association, Inc. Copyright © by the American Camping Association, Inc.

Arte Público Press—University of Houston. "Mirror, Mirror: Mambo No. 5" by Gustavo Pérez Firmat is reprinted with permission from the publisher of *Little Havana Blues: A Cuban-American Literary Anthology* (Houston: Arte Público Press—University of Houston, Copyright © 1996).

Brandt & Hochman Literary Agents, Inc. "Nancy Hanks" by Rosemary Carr and Stephen Vincent Benét, from *A Book of Americans* by Rosemary and Stephen Vincent Benét, copyright © 1933 by Rosemary and Stephen Vincent Benét. Copyright renewed © 1961 by Rosemary and Stephen Vincent Benét. Reprinted by permission of Brandt & Hochman Literary Agents, Inc.

Dial Books for Young Readers. From *Roll of Thunder, Hear My Cry* by Mildred D. Taylor, copyright © 1976 by Mildred D. Taylor. Used by permission of Dial Books for Young Readers, an imprint of Penguin Putnam Books for Young Readers, a division of Penguin Putnam Inc. and Penguin Books Ltd. All rights reserved.

Rita Dove. "Lady Freedom Among Us," from *On the Bus with Rosa Parks*, W. W. Norton, © 1999 by Rita Dove. Reprinted by permission of the author.

Dramatic Publishing Co. From *The Little Prince* by Rick Cummins and John Scoullar, based on the book *The Little Prince* by Antoine de Saint-Exupéry (available through Dramatic Publishing Co.).

EnchantedLearning.com. "Earth and the Milky Way," copyright © EnchantedLearning.com. Used by permission.

Headline Book Publishing Limited and John Wiley & Sons, Inc. Extracts from *Daughter of China* by Meihong Xu and Larry Engelmann. Copyright © 1999 Meihong Xu and Larry Engelmann. Reproduced by permission of Headline Book Publishing Limited and John Wiley & Sons, Inc.

Pearson Education, Inc. "Light," from *Prentice Hall Science Explorer: Focus on Physical Science* by Michael J. Padilla, Ph.D., Ioannis Miaoulis, Ph.D., and Martha Cyr, Ph.D. © 2001 by Pearson Education, Inc., publishing as Prentice Hall. Used by permission.

Pearson Education, Inc. "Why the Sun Is So High in the Heavens," from *World Myths and Legends II Mexico* by Flora Foss © 1993 by Globe Fearon. Used by permission of Pearson Education, Inc.

Martha Staid. "On van Gogh's *Starry Night*" by Martha Staid. Reprinted by permission of the author.

Steck-Vaughn Company. *Sor Juana Inés de la Cruz* by Kathleen Thompson. Copyright © 1993 Steck-Vaughn Company. Reprinted by permission.

Mandy Terc. "Sowing the Seeds of Peace" by Mandy Terc. In memory of the founder of Seeds of Peace, John Wallach, for his vision and the campers of Seeds of Peace, for their courage. Reprinted by permission of the author.

Windows to the Universe. "The Ten Chinese Suns" and "Re" adapted from Windows to the Universe, www.windowsucar.educar/.

Writers House. "I Have a Dream" by Martin Luther King Jr. Reprinted by arrangement with the Estate of Martin Luther King Jr., c/o Writers House as agent for the proprietor, New York, NY. Copyright © 1963 Dr. Martin Luther King Jr.; copyright renewed 1991 by Coretta Scott King.

Credits